A Garland Series

AMERICAN INDIAN ETHNOHISTORY
Plains Indians

compiled and edited by
DAVID AGEE HORR
Brandeis University

Kiowa-Commanche Indians

TRANSCRIPT OF HEARINGS OF
THE KIOWA, COMMANCHE,
AND APACHE TRIBES OF INDIANS
vs. THE UNITED STATES OF AMERICA

in two volumes
Volume II

COMMISSION FINDINGS
Indian Claims Commission

Garland Publishing Inc., New York & London
1974

Copyright © 1974

by Garland Publishing, Inc.

All Rights Reserved

Library of Congress Cataloging in Publication Data

```
United States. Indian Claims Commission.
   Transcript of hearings of the Kiowa, Commanche, and
Apache Tribes of Indians vs. the United States of
America.

   (American Indian ethnohistory:  Plains Indians)
   At head of title:  Kiowa-Commanche Indians.
   Vol. 2 includes Commission findings.
   Indian Claims Commission docket no. 32.
   1. Kiowa Indians--Claims.  2. Comanche Indians--
Claims.  3. Apache Indians--Claims.  I. Title.
II. Series.
KF8208.A845            343'.73'025           74-8378
ISBN 0-8240-0724-7
```

Printed in the United States of America

Contents

Volume I

Preface	7*
The Garland American Indian Ethnology Series	
General Nature and Content of the Series	
David Agee Horr	9
Indian Claims Commission, *Ralph A. Barney*	13
Introduction to the Ethnohistorical Reports on	
the Land Claims Cases, *Robert A. Manners*	17
Background Material on the Kiowa and Commanche Indians as of 1953	
Maps showing 1950 locations and estimated original ranges	20
Historical and Population Information	23
The Report	
Transcript of Hearings of the Kiowa, Commanche, and Apache Indians vs. the United States of America	27

Volume II

The Report Continued	7
Commission Findings, *Indian Claims Commission*	169

*Garland Publishing has repaginated this work (at outside center) to facilitate scholarly use. However, original pagination has been retained for internal reference.

TRANSCRIPT OF HEARINGS OF THE KIOWA,
COMMANCHE, AND APACHE TRIBES

OF INDIANS

vs.

THE UNITED STATES OF AMERICA

Volume II

Docket No. 32

PROCEEDINGS OF MAY 11, 1949.
commencing at 9:00 o'clock, a.m.

MR. THOMPSON: May it please the Court, before we start the testimony of our next witness, we feel that it would be an appropriate time to introduce some contemporary written evidence, which has a bearing upon the proceedings at this time. I offer, as the Plaintiffs' Exhibit No. 7, a letter signed by David H. Jerome, Chairman, to Honorable John W. Noble, Secretary of the Interior, dated October 7, 1892.

MR. BARNEY: No objection.

MR. THOMPSON: I would like to read this.

COMMISSIONER O'MARR: It may be admitted in evidence.

(Thereupon the said paper was by the Clerk marked as the Plaintiffs' Exhibit 7, for identification; which exhibit is included in "Book of Exhibits" at page numbered 11 thereof.)

MR. THOMPSON: You mean, it may be admitted without reading?

COMMISSIONER O'MARR: No, you may read it.

MR. THOMPSON: (Reading Exhibit 7) "Sir: Our negotiations with the Comanches, Kiowas and Apaches have nearly reached a conclusion" This is October 7, 1892.

COMMISSIONER O'MARR: I was looking for the date of that treaty.

MR. THOMPSON: The date is dated October 6th.

COMMISSIONER O'MARR: But it wasn't completed until about the 21st, if I remember?

MR. THOMPSON: That is correct.

MR. THOMPSON: (Reading) "Our negotiations with the Comanches, Kiowas and Apaches have nearly reached a conclusion, we having already secured one hundred and ninety-three signatures out of the four hundred and fifty required by their treaty of 1868." I may interpolate, that is the Medicine Lodge treaty. The date of its ratification. Back to the text. "The leading men of each tribe have signed the articles of agreement, and it seems now that our success is assured, but, in this opinion, we may possibly be mistaken. Last May (so Mr. Sayre reports to the Commission) you expressed to him your very decided opinion that with this relinquishment should also go the relinquishment of the pretended claim of the Choctaws and Chickasaws for this and the Wichita Country. We write now to inquire if this is yet your opinion, and to ask of you any specific advice you may choose to give in the premises. Answer at once, and by wire if you deem it prudent, as our labors here may end before an answer by mail could reach us. Very respectfully yours."

MR. THOMPSON: I offer as Plaintiffs' Exhibit 8 a photostatic copy, taken from the National archives, from the Press Copies that they used at that time, of the responding telegram, signed by John W. Noble, to David H. Jerome, and ask that this be admitted in evidence.

MR. BARNEY: No objection.

COMMISSIONER O'MARR: It will be received.

(The said exhibit, Plaintiffs' Exhibit No. 8, admitted in evidence, is included in the "Book of Exhibits" comprising a part of this transcript, at page number 12 thereof.)

MR. THOMPSON: I would like to read this. "October 12th, 1892. David H. Jerome, Chairman, Fort Sill, Oklahoma. Close on lowest terms possible in view of the claims of other Indians. There seems no other way. But Congress ought not to pay more than we will get back. Congratulate you on prospect completing your part." Signed: "John W. Noble, Secretary."

COMMISSIONER O'MARR: Who was Noble?

MR. THOMPSON: Secretary of the Interior, who had jurisdiction over the Office of Indian Affairs, as it then existed.

MR. THOMPSON: I offer, as Plaintiffs' Exhibit No. 9, a copy from the National Archives of a letter certified by James F. Randlett, Lt. Col., U.S.A., who was the United States Agent at the date of the certification, namely: January 5, 1900, which is a letter that was forwarded to the Indian Department on January 5, 1900, but which is dated October 11, 1892, and signed by Joshua Given and addressed to Rev. J.J. Methvin.

MR. BARNEY: No objection.

COMMISSIONER O'MARR: It may be received.

(The said exhibit, Plaintiffs' Exhibit 9, admitted in evidence, is included in the "Book of Exhibits" at page numbered 13 thereof.)

MR. THOMPSON: I would like to read this document. The letterhead is the "Office of Rice and Quinette, General Merchandise, Fort Sill, Oklahoma Territory. Fort Sill, Oklahoma, October 11th, 1892. Rev. J. J. Methvin, Anadarko, Oklahoma. My dear Friend: Yesterday, the Kiowas, Comanches and Apaches, through my efforts, adopted you, and consented to give you 160 acres of land for valuable services rendered them, through the four years you have been among them. I am very happy to tell you this news and I am sure you will be surprised greatly. I sincerly hope that you will pardon me for using your name in this connection, but on the other hand, you are given what you deserved. The three tribes in attendance of the Council wish you to accept this compliment. It is the expression of their good will toward you. I hope to see you soon. I am your friend. " Signed "Joshua Given," which letter, as I indicated, was not forwarded to the Department until 1900.

COMMISSIONER O'MARR: That was addressed to whom?

MR. THOMPSON: Rev. J. J. Methvin.

COMMISSIONER O'MARR: All right.

MR. THOMPSON: I next offer in evidence documents taken from the National Archives, and described as follows: Pages 1 --- strike that. By way of Explanation, Plaintiffs' Exhibit No. 9 is in the National Archives as 1-1 of a group of papers, indicating the time that it was forwarded. For convenience, I desire to separate this letter from the other letters and that will explain why the next offer I make starts with pages 1-2.

MR. THOMPSON: I offer, as the Plaintiffs' Exhibit No. 10, pages 1-2 through 1-7, inclusive, being papers taken from the National Archives of the following tenor: Pages 1-4 through 1-7, being a letter from James F. Randlett, U. S. Indian Agent, to the Commissioner of Indian Affairs in Washington, dated January 5, 1900, making reference to a memorial of protest which he is forwarding to Washington for consideration by Congress. It will have to be borne in mind, in this connection, that this treaty, though we are talking about it in 1892 - agreement, not treaty - was not ratified by Congress until June 6, 1900, a lapse of eight years, during which time there is considerable history. This letter which I have just referred to from Randlett to the Commissioner of Indian Affairs is dated January 5, 1900, prior to the ratification by Congress of the Jerome Agreement. Pages 1-2 and 1-3 are purportedly a copy of a protest signed by the Kiowa, Comanche and Apache Indians, under date of October 17th, 1892, at which time it will be remembered that the negotiations were still going forward. I shall not read this document into the record, but I would xx, for the purpose of the testimony this morning, make the following remarks concerning it. Perhaps, first, I better have it accepted into evidence.

MR. BARNEY: To which the defendant objects for the reason and on the ground that although it purports to be a protest, the copy offered shows, or fails to show, that it was signed by any one.

COMMISSIONER O'MARR: Is it a part of the official records?

MR. THOMPSON: The copy that is available now does not have appended to it any Indian signatures, or indication of consent. However, the letter which accompanies it and which forwarded it to Washington, is a full explanation as to how this document happened to repose in the files of the Indian Agent at Anadarko - this protest, for eight years without ever being brought to the attention of the authorities in Washington, and explains the absence of the signatures, and we request that it be admitted into evidence.

COMMISSIONER O'MARR: Where did you obtain the exhibit?

MR. THOMPSON: From the National Archives. It is a part of the departmental records.

COMMISSIONER O'MARR: Well, the objection is over-ruled.

MR. THOMPSON: I would, instead of reading the document into evidence - I would like to make a few remarks.

COMMISSIONER O'MARR: The exhibit is received in evidence.

(The said exhibit, Plaintiffs' Exhibit 10, is included in the "Book of Exhibits" at page __14__ thereof.)

MR. THOMPSON: This record indicates that Rev. J. J. Methvin, the individual who was adopted into the tribe through the courtesy of Joshua Givens, had this protest, dated October 7, 1892, in his hands, and as is indicated by Col. Randlett's letter, it was signed by more than four hundred adult males, Kiowa, Comanche and Apache Indians. According to this exhibit, Rev. Methvin approached the Indian Agent, Day, who, incidentally, it will be developed, also stood to gain an allotment from the Jerome Agreement. As will be indicated later on, he was included in Section 10, as an individual who would receive 160 acres of land. I notice the Commissioner is looking for it in the law. He will not find it there. It was removed. This document indicates that Agent Day stated, "You give the protest to me and I shall forward it to the attention of the proper authorities in Washington." That was in 1892. It is strange to say that the next we see of the document is when a new agent, in 1900, dredged it up out of the files of the Agency at Anadarko and thought that it should be brought to the attention of the authorities in Washington, and then was, for the first time, brought to the attention of any one in authority, outside of the local agent.

COMMISSIONER O'MARR: Incidentally, what was the protest?

MR. THOMPSON: The protest is contained in this document. It is pages 1-2 and 1-3. As a background and a basis for the next offer, I desire to invite the Commissioners' attention to Plaintiffs' Exhibit No. 6, by way of explanation of some of the testimony of yesterday, and by way of anticipation of the testimony today. I wish to invite the Commissioners' attention particularly to the proceedings of the Jerome Council, which start on page 8 of the Plaintiffs' Exhibit 6. Directing your attention to the bottom of page 11, you will note that there appears a statement by Quanah Parker, Comanche - I do not intend to read the statement, but I do invite the Commissioners' attention to his last statement where Quanah Parker says: "But now I want to know how much will be paid for one acre; what the terms will be, and when it will be paid." And Mr. Jerome's answer: "We will tell him that by and by." I also, in this same connection, would invite the Commissioners' attention to page 16, about two-thirds of the way down, at which time Quanah Parker states: "We do not all understand it, but I would like to know how many acres one individual is entitled to. The Medicine Lodge treaty indicates that 320 acres is what the head of a family is entitled to. I also want to know how much per acre." Mr. Jerome says: "We will tell you in a minute." On page 17, about one-third way down, Quanah Parker says again: "The Medicine Lodge treaty gives us 320 acres to the head of a family. You have not told us how much land you propose for one Indian to have, nor how much for one acre." On page 18, Quanah Parker says:

"One thing, how much per acre?" Mr. Sayre says: "I cannot tell you." Quanah Parker says: "How do you arrive at the number of millions of dollars if you do not know?" And Mr. Sayre says: "We just guess at it." Quanah Parker says, "We would like to know how much per acre, because we have heard that some tribes received a a $1.25 per acre, and the Wichitas received fifty cents per acre and were dissatisfied." On page 20, near the bottom of the page, Tabananaca, Comanche, says, in effect, "We want to know how much one acre of land is worth." And, as the Commissioners will observe, at about the center of page 21, we find for the first time a statement by the Commissioners that it is their best estimate that the land, they would receive about $1.10, or if certain acreage is included, it would be a trifle over a dollar.

MR. THOMPSON: Now, that is preferatory to this offer in evidence, which, incidentally, the method of the offer has been discussed with the government. In the National Archives appears the original of the proceedings which is printed in Plaintiffs' Exhibit 7 -- Plaintiffs' Exhibit 6. It is a long document, and in order to not unnecessarily expend the funds of the Indians, we have had abstracted from it page 115. This page pertains to a passage which occurs on page 48 of Plaintiffs' Exhibit 6, near the top of the page, where Big Tree, Kiowa, is speaking. This exhibit which I propose to offer is important to the plaintiffs' case, inasmuch as it goes to the issue of how much per acre was to be paid. You will note that on page 48 of Plaintiffs' Exhibit 6, Big Tree says, according to Plaintiffs' Exhibit 6: "I said I would want two million, five hundred thousand dollars." At this time, I offer in evidence, as the Plaintiffs' Exhibit 11, page 115, being the extract from the National Archives of the page which includes the passage by Big Tree on page 48 of Plaintiffs' Exhibit 6.

MR. BARNEY: No objection.

THE COMMISSIONER: It may be received.

MR. THOMPSON: Before leaving this exhibit, I would respectfully invite the Commissioners' attention to the figures $2,500,000 as it exists on the original record of Plaintiffs' Exhibit 11. It is plaintiffs' contention that the figures underneath, and which have been erased and over which $2,500,000 has been superimposed were $2.50 per acre.

(The Plaintiffs' Exhibit No. 11, admitted in evidence as shown above, is included in "Book of Exhibits" at page number **15** thereof.)

MR. THOMPSON: May we proceed with our next witness?

COMMISSIONER O'MARR: Yes, you may proceed.

TSING TON KEAH (Hunting Horse) called as a witness by plaintiffs, being first duly sworn to testify truth, the whole truth and nothing but truth (through interpreter) testified through the interpreter, Rev. Pauahty, previously sworn as interpreter, as follows:

(NOTE BY REPORTER: Where questions are directed to the witness in the third person, such as, "Ask him whether," etc., it is to be understood that the questioner was talking to the interpreter and directing him to ask the witness a certain question; and where the answer is given in the third person, such as, "He said," etc., it is to be understood that the interpreter interpreted the question to the witness and the witness answered in his native tongue which answer was then interpreted in the third person, such as, "He said his name is John Jones."

DIRECT EXAMINATION
QUESTIONS BY MR. MISKOVSKY:

Q You may state your name.

A Tsing-ton keah. White name "Hunting Horse."

Q What is your enrolled Indian name?

A Tsing ton keah is his Indian name.

    REPORTER: How is that spelled?

    INTERPRETER: T-s-a-t-b-k-e.

Q What is your age?

A About 103 years.

Q Can you read, write or speak the English language?

A No, sir.

Q Did you ever attend school?

A   Yes, I attended school just a short while, but due to the war broke out I was forced to quit.

Q   What war do you have reference to?

A   This disturbance he mentioned was during the time that some riot took place among the Comanches, near Lawton. That is what he has in mind.

Q   What was he doing as a young man?

A   My life was nomadic and I have no permanent dwelling place. I just roam all over the Indian country.

Q   Was he ever in the army or employed by the United States government during his early manhood?

A   Yes, he was a member of the Indian soldiers here at Ft. Sill.

Q   Well, what did he do?

A   We are to guard any disturbance in the Indian Country and then where any lawlessness is within the Indian Country we are sent out to investigate and to enforce peace within the Indian Country.

Q   Now, was he a scout for the soldiers that were stationed at Ft. Sill?

A   He is not clear, but he said that he belonged to the United States army. He didn't say a scout, but I presume that is what he meant.

Q   Did he know what the boundaries of the Kiowa, Comanche and Apache reservation were when he served as a scout, or was associated with the army?

A   He only remembers any indication of the boundary is near Chickasha on the east, on the south to Quanah and he does not remember the boundary line on the west, but it is a vast territory.

Q   Now, does he remember when the Jerome Commission came to this immediate vicinity?

A   Yes, he heard they came.

Q   Did he know where they met when they arrived upon the reservation?

A   He does not know where the Council was held.

Q   Did he attend any of the Council meetings at Ft. Sill or at Anadarko?

A   He did not attend.

Q   Did he sign, or ever have presented to him for his signature, the Jerome Agreement?

A   Yes, he signed it.

Q   He signed the Jerome Agreement?

A   The agreement, he said he signed it with the understanding, as it was interpreted to him.

Q   Who requested him to sign or place his name upon the Jerome Agreement?

A   He said, "I signed because I supported Quanah Parker's proposition."

Q   Now, will he tell us, please, what Quanah Parker's proposition was?

A   I signed because I understood that Quanah Parker opposed the allotting of the territory.

Q   Now, ask him this question, please, sir: Did he sign the agreement, the Jerome Agreement, or a protest to the Jerome Agreement?

INTERPRETER: I think he answered that.

Q   Ask him where he had his signature placed upon the instrument that he signed.

A   Near Fort Sill. Of course, he described the place.

Q   What was the description that he gave?

A   Oil refinery, I suppose, now, or near Fort Sill.

Q   Now, at the time that he affixed his mark, or his signature, what was his understanding as to what the Indians were to receive?

A   I signed the agreement because I believed that was the best.

Q   Now, was the Commission in session, the white men with the Indians, at the time that his signature was placed upon the agreement?

INTERPRETER: You mean whether the Commission was there?

Q   Yes.

A   I signed in the presence of Quanah Parker and his wife and Sam Quoetone.

Q   Was Joshua Givens there?

A   He was not present.

Q   Was there any white men present?

A   It was in the presence of Quanah Parker and his wife and Sam Quoetone, and a few Comanches, but Joshua Givens was not present.

Q   Now, could he write his own name?

A   No, sir.

Q   Ask him if when Chief Quanah Parker asked him to sign the agreement if he placed a pencil or a pen in his hand and asked him to mark an "x" beside his name.

A   No, Quanah Parker did not.

Q   Well, did anybody else there do that? Did Sam Quoetone or Quanah Parker's wife ask him to make his signature by an "x"?

A   It was Sam Quoetone that had him to hold the pen and then sign his name.

Q   Did he ever, after he signed the Jerome Agreement, ever sign a protest or complain to any one and ask his name be withdrawn?

A   He did not sign.

Q   He did not sign a protest?

A   He only signed one time and that was when he signed the agreement with Sam Quoetone.

Q   Of what Indian tribe is he a member?

A   He is half Kiowa and his mother was a captive, and he is only one-half.

Q   That is all.

       MR. BARNEY: No questions.
       WITNESS EXCUSED

(Witness Luther Sahmaunt called to the stand and Mrs. Ioleta McElhaney called and sworn by the clerk as interpreter, and thereupon the witness was sworn by the clerk through said interpreter.)

LUTHER SAHMAUNT, called as a witness by plaintiffs, being first duly sworn, as above stated, testified through said interpreter, as follows:

(NOTE BY REPORTER: Where questions are directed to the witness in the third person, such as "Ask him whether," etc., it is to be understood that the questioner was talking to the interpreter and directing him to ask the witness a certain question; and where the answer is given in the third person, such as, "He said, etc., it is to be understood that the interpreter interpreted the question to the witness and then interpreted the answer of the witness in the third person, such as, "My name is John Jones," would be interpreted as "He said his name is John Jones.")

DIRECT EXAMINATION

QUESTIONS BY MR. MISKOVSKY:

Q   You may state your name.

A   Luther Sahmaunt.

Q   Do you have a given name?

A   Luther.

Q   From what - Of what tribe of Indians are you a member?

A   Kiowa.

Q   What is your age?

A   Eighty-seven.

Q   Do you remember the Jerome Commission coming to the Kiowa, Comanche and Apache reservation?

A   Yes.

Q   Do you remember about when that was?

A   He doesn't know the year, but he knows when they came.

Q   Were you married about that time?

A   Yes.

Q   Of what did your family consist?

A   Four children.

Q   What was your age at that time?

A   He doesn't know exactly. Over twenty.

Q   Where were you residing about that time?

A   He said he lived at Mount Scott - near Mount Scott at the time. He was working at Anadarko.

Q   What was he doing at Anadarko and by whom was he employed?

A   He was working for the Agency.

Q   What was the nature of his work?

A   He had various duties. Sometimes outside work.

Q   Did he ever assist the government in distributing rations?

A   Yes.

Q   Does he remember the time that the Jerome Commission came to Anadarko?

A   Yes.

Q   Did he attend any of the meetings that were held there by the Commission?

A   He didn't attend all the meetings. He came about noon and attended some of the time.

Q   Now then, there is one question I want to preface that with. Ask him to state whether or not the distribution of rations was made prior to the arrival of the Jerome Commission or subsequent to their arrival by the government to the Indians?

A   He doesn't know for certain.

Q   As I understood him, he stated that he attended an afternoon meeting of the council, is that right?

A   He arrived there just before noon, before the session dismissed.

Q   Ask him approximately how long he was there in attendance before the session recessed. How long was he there before it recessed?

A   He doesn't give the time, but it was just a short time and he said he was late to the meeting.

Q   Where was the meeting being held?

A   He said it was a warehouse next to the Ration House building. This building was used that was south of the Ration building where they kept the ration supplies.

Q   Now, have him tell us who of the Kiowa chiefs were present when he was there just before noon.

A   When he arrived, Big Tree was speaking, and Ahpeatone was standing, and Joshua Givens was standing. The rest was seated facing the other way and I don't know who they were. There were a lot of folks there.

Q   Was he near enough to Big Tree that he could relate what he was saying -- strike that. Did he know the names of any of the Commissioners that were present, if there were any present?

A   I do not know their names, but there were three.

Q   Now, did he hear Big Tree make any statement there at the meeting to either the Commissioners or to Joshua Givens?

A   Yes.

Q   Have him to relate, as nearly as he can, the substance of Big Tree's conversation with Joshua Givens.

A   Big Tree said to Joshua Givens, "You know that they have cheated us and why do you say they did not." Joshua answered him and said, "They haven't cheated you," and Big Tree said, "Yes, they did. If they did not cheat us, let us see the papers." "No, we will not let you see them," was the reply of Joshua to Big Tree.

Q   Now, did he hear anything else that was said there?

A   Big Tree told him, he said, "All right, you said they did not cheat us, if it is so, raise your hand, and if it is so one of us will die. If you are telling the truth, then I will die, and if I am telling the truth, you will die." The expression is "You will fall outstretched." It is just an expression which would mean death.

Q   Does he remember anything else that was said?

A   No one else said anything, but my impression was that they were suspicious of being defrauded and so they said

"Let us go."

Q   Did he attend a meeting that was held in the afternoon, if one was held?

A   No. As far as he knows, there wasn't any meeting.

Q   Were any signatories being requested at the meeting that he attended, to the Jerome Agreement?

A   He doesn't know.

Q   Did you sign the Jerome Agreement?

A   No.

Q   That is all.

   MR. BARNEY: No questions.

WITNESS EXCUSED

(Rev. Pauahty, the first interpreter used, was called to act as interpreter for the next witness.)

ODLE PAH QUOIT, called as a witness by the plaintiffs, being first duly sworn to testify truth, the whole truth and nothing but truth, testified through said interpreter as follows:

(NOTE BY REPORTER: See statement by reporter as to questions and answers asked and answered in the third person heretofore made.)

DIRECT EXAMINATION

QUESTIONS BY MR. MISKOVSKY:

Q   What is your name?

A   Odle pah quoit.

Q   And that is also your enrolled name?
A   Yes. English name, White Fox.
Q   What is your age?
A   About 83 years old.
Q   Of what Indian tribe are you a member?
A   Kiowa.
Q   Do you remember the Commission coming to the Kiowa, Comanche and Apache reservation?
A   Yes.
Q   Approximately what was your age at that time, if you know?
A   About 22 years of age.
Q   Do you know where the Council held its meetings?
A   I heard a meeting was held near Fort Sill, but I did not go.
Q   Was there a meeting held other than at Fort Sill?
A   Yes.
Q   Where was it held?
A   Anadarko.
Q   Did you attend any of the meetings at Anadarko?
A   Yes, I attended. I attended the Anadarko council.
Q   Do you know about when that was?
A   I do not remember, but somewhere near sixty years ago - somewhere - not yet sixty years.
Q   Do you remember the names of any Kiowa chiefs who were in attendance at this meeting?

203

A   Lone Wolf, Komalty, Big Tree, he remembers particularly those three.

Q   Does he know whether or not Joshua Givens was there?

A   Yes, he was.

Q   Were any of the troops, or soldiers, in attendance at that meeting?

A   There was a large crowd there, but I remember there were some soldiers there.

Q   Were any white men there?

A   He remembers only three, the members of the Commission.

Q   Did he know their names?

A   I do not understand English and I do not know their names. I have not learned their names.

Q   Did he see or talk with Joshua Givens prior to this council meeting there?

A   No, sir.

Q   When did you attend the meeting? Was it before noon or afternoon?

A   The meeting was not very long. It commenced just a little before noon and it didn't last very long.

Q   When he arrived, who was talking, if any one?

A   Big Tree and Joshua Givens.

Q   Have him state, as nearly as he can, what was being said by Big Tree and Joshua Givens.

A   I remember particularly the statement of Joshua Givens.

Joshua Givens wanted to know whether the people were ready to sign the Jerome Agreement, or the agreement, and then Big Tree replied, and, of course, you understand that Joshua Givens was representing the Commission, and Big Tree replied to Joshua Givens and requested that the contents of the agreement shall be interpreted and explained more clearly to the people, and Joshua Givens, who was interpreting for the Commission, interpreted to Big Tree and said that the papers were not available and that they cannot see them, that they already had been mailed to Washington. Big Tree asked Joshua Givens that they wanted $2.50 per acre for the land that the government want to buy and they do not want to sell it for less than that price, and, Joshua Givens, you have not made yourself clear and the Commission have not been clear in interpreting the contents of the agreement and we are suspicious and we are afraid that there is something about this thing, that you refuse to furnish us with the interpretation and we are afraid that there is something wrong or you would be open and interpret the agreement to us and to the people. Then Big Tree said to Joshua Givens that if there is any miscarriage of justice, or if the truth has not been told, there is a divine penalty, as far as the Indians know, that it always brings death, and if you have told us the truth, then I would die first, but if you are wrong and have hid the truth from us, then you will die first.

Then it developed into a personal hot argument between the two men. They got personal after those statements were made.

Q Does he have anything further he wants to say?

A White fox (witness) just added this out of his own heart. "If there is anything that have been taken away from our people, or I hope and trust that if there is anything that has been unjustly taken from us, or our people has been deprived of, I only trust and ask that the things that have been taken from us unjustly be restored. I only ask for the things that should have been mine, and if it has been unjustly taken away from my people, all I want is to have it restored back to us, and nothing more.

32 Q I wish you would ask the witness, did Joshua Givens ask any one to sign?

A You mean, in the council?

Q Yes.

A I remember that Joshua did ask our people to sign the agreement and I heard that he went about from camp to camp, tent to tent, procuring signatures. I heard that. But the majority of the people did not want to sign, but nevertheless he went about to procure signatures.

Q Did you sign the agreement?

A I did not sign.

Q That is all with this witness.

CROSS EXAMINATION

QUESTIONS BY MR. BARNEY:

How many sessions of the council were there held at Anadarko?

A   I attended only one session and that was at Anadarko and there were no other councils or meetings held as far as I remember. I went on home.

Q   During the council that you heard, did the white Commissioners say anything at all?

A   I want to tell the truth. None of the white men of the Commission spoke, but Joshua Givens was the interpreter and he speaks for the Commission and so, therefore, there was no need for them to get up and speak, because they spoke in Kiowa.

Q   Didn't they speak, the Commissioners, if they had anything to say to the people - didn't they say it like I am talking to you, through an interpreter, either to some one of the Kiowas or Comanches? Wasn't that the way the council was held, just like we are talking, through an interpreter now?

A   I only remember what I see, but they maybe one time speak before I arrived, but during my presence, none of the Commissioners spoke through their interpreter. Their interpreter, their official interpreter, spoke for them. The official interpreter being Joshua Givens.

Q   Do you remember three men being sworn as interpreters that day?

A   He does not remember any interpreter sworn, only Joshua was interpreting.

Q   Ask him - I want to see if he understands - Ask him if he remembers, or understands that this white man Jerome was the head of this Commission. See if he understands or remembers that.

A   He can only describe them - physical description. "One had grey hair - very grey hair; one was writing on a paper, and one was middle-age man, or little past middle age man, but I do not know their names. I cannot distinguish them by their names."

Q   Do you remember at the Anadarko meeting of Ahpeatone being present at the meeting?

A   He does not remember Ahpeatone present.

Q   You do not remember that Ahpeatone and one of the Commissioners had big words like Joshua Givens had with Big Tree? You don't remember that?

A   I don't remember any one only just what I witnesses in the council at Anadarko.

Q   And the only talks he can remember is the discussion or quarrel between Big Tree and Joshua Givens?

A   I remember particularly the personal argument between the two men because it was so conspicuous, you know, in the large crowd, and perhaps other things was said previous to the two men quarreling.

Q   Did that quarrel take place in the council meeting itself or at some other place?

A   It took place at the council.

Q   In the council meeting?

A   Yes.

Q   Right in the middle of the session, while the session was going on?

A   Yes, that was during the session. It was because of the inquiry Big Tree made and the reply that Givens made that created it.

Q   Did the council break up right after that?

A   He heard the words of Big Tree that they wanted $2.50 per acre and we don't want anything else and if we cannot get that, then we don't want to discuss it, and so he told every one to disperse and go back to their homes.

Q   Who did?

A   Big Tree.

Q   Big Tree is the man who told everybody to disperse and go home?

A   Yes, sir.

    INTERPRETER: He added on there "unless they agreed and if they did, we will meet again," That is the last sentence. I left that out.

Q   Let me understand that.

A   "Unless they agreed to do that and then we will meet again."

Q   Did the council meet again?

A   I do not remember any meeting after that meeting. If I had heard of any meeting, I would have tried to attend, but I went right on back to my home.

Q   That is all.

WITNESS EXCUSED

(MRS. McELHANEY called and sworn as an interpreter by the Clerk.)

TONEMAH, called as a witness on the part of plaintiffs, being first duly sworn, through said interpreter, to testify truth, the whole truth and nothing but truth, testified as follows:

(NOTE BY REPORTER: See statement by reporter previously made as to questions and answers asked and answered in the third person.)

DIRECT EXAMINATION

QUESTIONS BY MR. MISKOVSKY:

Q   State your name.

A   Tonemah.

Q   Do you have a given name?

A   When he was a boy, he had another name, "Yellow Boy."

Q   Is Tonemah his enrolled Indian name?

A   Yes, sir.

Q   What is your age?

A   He had a boyhood name, "Yellow Boy Tonemah" is the only name he used.

Q   What is your age?

A   76.

Q   Of what tribe of Indians are you a member?

A   Kiowa.

Q   As a young man, what did he do?

A   I didn't do anything in particular. I didn't go to school and just lived with my folks.

Q   Later on did he become a member of the United States army?

A   Yes, sir,

Q   When?

A   1892.

Q   Does he have his discharge upon his person?

A   Yes.

   INTERPRETER: I have it for him.

   MR. MISKOVSKY: May I see it, please? (Paper handed to Mr. Miskovsky by interpreter.)

Q   How long did you serve in the army of the United States?

A   Three years.

Q   And what was your rank?

A   Corporal.

Q   Now, where were you stationed?

A   Fort Sill.

Q   What troop were you a member of?

A   "L" troop.

Q   Were you in the calvary or artillery?

A   Calvery.

Q   Do you read and write or speak the English language?

A   I never went to school, but I do know how to write my name.

Q   Do you understand English to a limited extent?

A   Yes.

Q   Now, who was your immediate commanding officer when you were attached to "L" troop, Seventh Calvary?

A   He was Lt. Scott, later Captain Scott.

Q   Is that Captain Hugh L. Scott?

A   Yes, H. L. Scott.

Q   H. L.?

A   Or Hugh L.

Q   Were you married or single?

A   Married.

Q   Of what did your family consist?

A   Two

Q   Do you remember the Jerome Commission coming upon the reservation, that is, the Kiowa, Comanche and Apache reservation?

A   Yes.

Q   Do you know where the Commission met?

A   They met at the Comanche store. The Commissioners stayed at the Fort.

Q   Where at the Fort?

A   Officers quarters. They stayed in the officers' quarters.

Q   Now, did you attend any of the hearings while the Commission was at or near Fort Sill?

A   Yes.

Q   Where was it near Fort Sill?

A   The Red Store.

Q   Was that near Fort Sill?

A   Near Fort Sill.

Q   Now, who was in attendance the day - strike that, please. Will you name the Kiowa Chiefs that were present the day you were in attendance?

A   Lone Wolf, Komalty and Big Tree.

Q   Now, what was said by the Commissioners, if anything, about the agreement and what the purpose of the Commission at the reservation was?

A   He heard the interpreter relate that they were to get 160 acres and the surplus land to be sold and paid in money and I couldn't get him to say that he heard the interpreter.

Q   Did he know what else the agreement contained?

A   He doesn't know.

Q   Were there any signatories requested by the Commission to the agreement when he was there?

A   No, he doesn't remember, but he goes on to say that later they did sign in their barracks.

Q   He did sign it in the barracks?

A   Yes, sir.

Q   Did he attend any other council meetings than the one I have inquired about?

A   No, he was in the army and he was stationed at Fort Sill and he stayed there.

Q   Did he later go to Anadarko?

A   No.

Q   Where did he sign his name to the Jerome Agreement?

A   In his quarters, the quarters of "L" troop.

Q   Who brought the agreement by to have him sign it?

A   Joshua did.

Q   Who else was present with Joshua Givens?

A   There were several there. Some were on duty, and he doesn't name any one in particular.

Q   Were there any members of the Commission there?

A   Different ones were on duty at different times. Joshua carried the papers. They must have given him the duty to do that.

Q   Did he sign his name to the agreement in his own handwriting or did he sign it by marking an "x" opposite his name?

A   He signed his name.

Q   Ask him at this time to take this pencil -- (interrupted)

    MR. THOMPSON: Let's do it with pen and ink.

Q   -- take this pen and sign his name.

(Witness writes name on paper handed him by counsel)

BY MR. MISKOVSKY: At this time, if Your Honors please, we desire to introduce the signature of the witness as it has been affixed to the paper which I hold in my hand and mark it as Plaintiffs' Exhibit 12. (Paper containing signature of witness so marked by clerk.)

COMMISSIONER O'MARR: It may be received.

(The said exhibit, Plaintiffs' Exhibit 12, admitted in evidence as shown above, is included in "Book of Exhibits," at page number 16 thereof)

Q   Now, direct his attention to the signature that appears opposite number 318 on Plaintiffs' Exhibit 5, and ask him if that signature which appears there upon this instrument is his name and in his handwriting.

A   Yes.

Q   Now, direct his attention to the "x" and "His mark" and ask him if he affixed his mark opposite his name at the time that he signed this instrument.

A   He doesn't remember signing that.

Q   Now, how old a man were you at the time that your signature appears upon this agreement - or that you signed the agreement?

A   I was twenty-five.

Q   Did you later talk to Joshua Givens about your name

being upon the Jerome Agreement?

A   Later I talked to Joshua and asked him what difference would one name make, that I wanted my name taken off, erased.

Q   What did Joshua Givens say to you about taking your name off, if anything?

INTERPRETER: I didn't translate awhile ago all he said. Just before this, he said, "I have made a mistake and I want my name taken off," and then Joshua told him, "You have done right." He said, "We will leave your signature on there. You have done right."

Q   Now, have him tell us when he requested Joshua Givens to take his name off with reference to how long it was after he signed this agreement?

A   Same day - later on in the same day.

Q   And did Joshua Givens tell him that his name would be taken off of there?

A   No.

Q   Did you ever see Joshua Givens after that time?

A   I seen him later, but it was useless to ask him any more about having my name taken off.

Q   Did you see him in your quarters after you had signed this?

A   He said Joshua was seated at a table in the quarters and as each member of "L" troop came in, he asked them to sign. He said, "When I came in, he said for me to come and sit down and he talked to me very kindly and asked me to sign and I did.

Q   Was that the first time?

A   The first time.

Q   Was Joshua Givens taking signatures in the barracks?

A   In the barracks.

Q   Now, did Captain Scott ever talk to the members of "L" troop about the Jerome Agreement?

A   Captain Scott urged us not to sign and later when he asked us if we had signed and we told him we had, he told me, "I am very sorry."

Q   Now, do you know about how many days that was after you signed the agreement that you heard this statement made by Lt. or Captain Scott?

A   The same day.

Q   The same day?

A   The same day.

Q   Now, did he later sign a protest to the Jerome Agreement?

A   No.

Q   Did you ever attend any other meetings that the Council or Commission held, other than the one you have told us about?

A   No.

Q   I take it that you didn't attend any of the meetings at Anadarko, is that correct?

A   No, I did not attend.

Q   Did you sign your name to the pay-roll when you were

a member of "L" troop when you were paid?

A   Yes, I signed my name.

Q   You may cross examine.

       MR. BARNEY: No questions.

       WITNESS EXCUSED

       COMMISSIONER O'MARR: We will take a recess until 1:30, Gentlemen.

(Thereupon this hearing was recessed until the hour of 1:30 o'clock, p.m., and at said hour this hearing was resumed with all officers, and counsel, present as at the time of recessing. And further proceedings were had as follows, to-wit:)

    BY MR. MISKOVSKY: With the permission of the Commission, at this time the plaintiffs would like to recall Mr. Tonemah to the stand.

       COMMISSIONER O'MARR: Very well.

(Thereupon the interpreter Mrs. McElhaney was recalled to act as interpreter.)

TONEMAH, the witness on the stand at the time of recessing for the noon meal, recalled to the witness stand, testified further as follows:

DIRECT EXAMINATION BY MR. MISKOVSKY:

Q   Your name is Tonemah?

A   Yes, sir (witness answering in English without aid of interpreter.)

Q   And you are the same Tonemah who testified before the noon recess?

A   Yes.

Q   Before the noon recess, I handed you an instrument and asked you if your name and signature appeared upon it?

A   Yes. (witness answering direct in English)

Q   Did you understand my question?

A   Ask me again.

Q   Did you understand my question, whether this writing upon this instrument which appears opposite 318 is your name and signature?

A   Yes.

Q   Now, I will ask you to again examine the signature opposite 318 and state to the Commission whether or not that is in your handwriting. Is that your handwriting?

A   No, I do not write my name like that.

Q   That is all. You may cross examine.

CROSS EXAMINATION

QUESTIONS BY MR. BARNEY:

Q   Whose handwriting is it?

A   I do not know who wrote it.

Q   When Joshua Givens came into the barracks and txx talked with you, you told him that you would sign the paper, didn't you?

A   I don't offer to write. He came to me and asked me to write in the kindest of words and under persuasion.

Q   Well, you did tell him all right?

A   Yes, I consented to sign. Soon after I signed it, the same day, I went to him and asked him to take my name off. I realized that I had done wrong. Some would sign and some refused, and I realized I had done a wrong and asked him to take my name off. I said, "Why should you worry over my signature. I am just one person. Take it off," but he refused.

Q   Did not Tonemah (witness) say this morning that Joshua said "No, you have done right and Tonemah said 'All right'"?

A   I wanted my name off and he refused and I gave up. He said I did right, but I wanted my name off.

Q   Did he see Joshua Givens, or anybody else, sign his name to this paper?

A   Yes, he saw Joshua write his name.

Q   Did he touch the pen to his mark?

A   He is not clear on that.

Q   That is all.

WITNESS EXCUSED

COMMISSIONER O'MARR: I think the record should show that the signature mentioned by the last witness is that contained in Exhibit No. 5 at 318.

(Rev. Pauahty, having heretofore been sworn as an interpreter, called to act as interpreter for the next witness.)

OTIS TSOTIGH, called on behalf of the plaintiffs, being, through said interpreter, first duly sworn to testify truth, the whole truth and nothing but truth, testified through said interpreter as follows:

(NOTE BY REPORTER: See previous explanation of reporter with respect to questions directed to the witness through the interpreter in the third person, such as, "Ask him," etc., and answers by the witness interpreted in the third person, such as "He said," etc.)

DIRECT EXAMINATION

QUESTIONS BY MR. MISKOVSKY:

Q   You may state your name.

A   Otis Tsotigh.

Q   What Indian tribe are you a member of?

A   Kiowa.

Q   Is Otis Tsotigh your enrolled Indian name?

A   Yes.

Q   What is your age?

A   72 years.

Q   Do you remember the Jerome Commission coming to the Kiowa, Comanche and Apache reservation?

A   Yes, I heard they came.

Q   Did you attend any of the meetings?

      INTERPRETER: What do you mean?

Q   Any of the Council meetings of the Jerome Commission?

A   He attended only one and that was the meeting at Anadarko.

Q   Now, can he tell us who of the Kiowa tribe was present at the Anadarko meeting when he attended, of the chiefs?

A   He said there were several Kiowa war chiefs who were present, but he remembers particularly Big Tree and Komalty and Lone Wolf.

Q   Was he present at the Council meeting when Lone Wolf was addressing the Commission?

A   Yes.

Q   Did he talk to Lone Wolf the day he attended the Council meeting?

A   Yes, he heard him.

Q   Where did he talk to Lone Wolf?

A   I heard him at the group of Kiowas at the camp in Anadarko.

Q   What did Lone Wolf state, if anything, with reference to the Jerome Agreement?

A   He only heard the statement that Lone Wolf made and reported to the group of Kiowas at this camp, that the Indians asked $2.50 per acre for the sale of their land and he believed that that was the price that all the Indians ought to agree to. He heard him make that statement.

Q   Were signatories to the agreement requested by any one at the Council, or anywhere else, during that day?
A   At this particular time he is at the camp now?
Q   That is right.
    INTERPRETER: Is that what you are referring to?
Q   Either at the camp or at the council?
A   No, sir.
Q   Did you sign the Jerome Agreement?
A   No, sir.
Q   Why did you not sign it?
A   He heard Lone Wolf make the statement that $2.50 per acre was the price that he thought was right, and he agreed with Lone Wolf and that was the reason he did not sign.
Q   You may cross examine.

CROSS EXAMINATION

QUESTIONS BY MR. BARNEY:

Q   You didn't sign the agreement because the Indians wanted $2.50 an acre, but that was not what the agreement called for, is that right?
A   Yes - not that alone, but some other things that I didn't think it was right for me to accept and sign, and not only the price.
Q   All right, we will go into that in a minute. I just want to get his answer clear. The Indians thought they should have $2.50 an acre, but that wasn't what the agreement said and that was one reason he didn't sign, is that right?

A   He did not sign because Lone Wolf reported to the group of Kiowas at the camp that that was the price that they asked for the sale of their land and Lone Wolf made that statement at the camp and so I heard the statement and I agreed with Lone Wolf.

Q   Lone Wolf said that the Indians wanted $2.50 an acre but the Commission, the Jerome Commission, was not willing to give that amount of money, and that is the reason he didn't sign the Jerome Agreement, is that right?

A   No, he did not sign because that the price of the land, he feels that it is not enough for the surplus land that was to be sold.

Q   What did you understand the Commission was willing to pay for the surplus land?

A   He heard that the Commission offered only a dollar, or somewhere thereabout, per acre, and he felt that was not enough for the price of their land.

Q   And that was the reason he didn't sign the agreement?

A   He followed the public sentiment of his people that he wants to follow and did not sign.

Q   That is all.

    MR. MISKOVSKY: Does the Commission desire to ask this witness any question?

    COMMISSIONER O'MARR: No, sir.

    WITNESS EXCUSED

WIND GOOMBA, called on the part of plaintiffs, being first duly sworn, through the interpreter, to testify truth, the whole truth and nothing but truth, testified through interpreter Rev. Pauahty, as follows:

(NOTE BY REPORTER: See previous explanation of reporter with respect to questions directed to the witness through the interpreter in the third person, such as "Ask him," etc., and answers by the witness interpreted in the third person, such as "He said," etc.)

DIRECT EXAMINATION

QUESTIONS BY MR. MISKOVSKY:

Q You may state your name.
A Goomba.
Q Do you have a given name - first name?
A Wind.
Q Of what Indian tribe are you a member?
A Kiowa.
Q Is Wind Goomba your enrolled name?
A Yes, that is my enrolled name.
Q What is your age?
A 81 years of age.
Q Do you remember the Jerome Commission coming to the Kiowa, Comanche and Apache reservation?
A Yes, I heard they came.
Q What was your age at that time?

A 23 years of age.

Q Was he married or single?

A Yes, he was married.

Q Of what did his family consist?

A Two children.

Q Did he attend any of the meetings of the Council when they were in session upon the reservation?

A He did not attend any of the Council.

Q Did he and his family receive allotments?

A Yes.

Q How many allotments did his family receive?

A He wants to make a correction. There was three children instead of two. They received five allotments.

Q Where were those allotments selected?

A Around Mountain View.

Q How many acres did they receive in each allotment?

A 160 acres.

Q Does he still own his allotment?

A No. I do not have my original allotment.

Q Was his original allotment sold?

A Yes, I sold mine.

Q How many acres was sold - strike that, please. As I understand it, his original allotment consisted of 160 acres, is that correct?

A Yes, sir.

Q   And he no longer has that 160 acre allotment?

A   I sold that.

Q   How was that allotment sold?

A   I sold my allotment about fifteen years ago.

Q   Was it sold through the Indian Agency at Anadarko?

A   He received the patent and the allotment and sold it.

Q   What did he receive for his allotment at the time it was sold?

A $12,000.00.

Q   Does his wife still own her allotment?

A   The City of Mountain View purchased that land from her.

Q   Does he know when the City of Mountain View purchased that allotment?

A   About forty years ago.

Q   How much of the allotment was sold to the City of Mountain View?

A   We received ten thousand dollars for 80 acres of her allotment.

Q   Now, does the family still own the remainder, the remaining three quarters and 80 acres of the allotments?

A   You mean of these two allotments?

Q   Of the five.

A   Yes, we have the remaining 80 acres of my wife's allotment and the allotments that were given to my children, still in trust.

Q   His wife's allotment was sold through the Indian Agency, the same as his allotment was sold, is that correct?

A   Through the Indian Office supervision of the sale of his wife's allotment.

Q   You may cross examine.

MR. BARNEY: No questions.

COMMISSIONER O'MARR: You will be excused.

WITNESS EXCUSED

MR. MISKOVSKY: I would like to announce, if Your Honors please, that these are all the Kiowas who will testify that we know of at this time, and we are about ready to start calling the witnesses who will appear as members of the Comanche tribe, and if it would be convenient, we would like to have a recess at this time for a few minutes.

COMMISSIONER O'MARR: How much time do you want?

MR. MISKOVSKY: I would say ten minutes, if Your Honor please, so we can see who our interpreters will be for the Comanche tribe.

COMMISSIONER O'MARR: Advise us when you are ready, will you, please.

MR. MISKOVSKY: Yes, sir.

(Thereupon a recess was had of about fifteen minutes, at the end of which time this hearing was resumed with all officers and counsel present as before, and further proceedings were had as follows, to-wit:)

(Rev. Robert Choot called to act as interpreter and being first duly sworn by the clerk to act as such interpreter, took a seat near the witness stand.)

BY MR. MISKOVSKY: If Your Honors please, the interpreter who is acting at this time is Rev. Robert Choot, and he is a member of the Reform Church in America, and he has lived all his life among the Comanches and has spoken Comanche throughout his entire life. Is that correct:

INTERPRETER CHOOT: Yes, I am a Comanche.

CODY NAH, called as a witness on the part of plaintiffs, being first, through said interpreter, duly sworn to testify truth, the whole truth and nothing but truth, testified through said interpreter as follows:

55

(NOTE BY REPORTER: See explanation of reporter heretofore made in this record with reference to questions asked in the third person and answers interpreted in the third person.)

DIRECT EXAMINATION

QUESTIONS BY MR. MISKOVSKY:

Q   You may state your name.
A   Cody nah.
Q   Now, it is spelled another way in Comanche, isn't that true?
A   INTERPRETER: Yes, I do not know the exact spelling. It has a "K" instead of a "C", I think.

Q   Well, the name is also spelled another way in Comanche, is that correct?

A   Yes, sir.

Q   And that spelling is Kah den na?

A   Yes, sir.

Q   What is your age?

A   78.

Q   You will have to speak up so the Commissioners may hear your answer and, second, so the reporter can record the answers into the record. Of what Indian tribe are you a member?

A   Comanche.

Q   Do you remember when the Jerome Commission came upon the Kiowa, Comanche and Apache reservation?

A   He says he was there but he doesn't remember the date and has no way of telling the exact date.

Q   Where did the Commission hold its hearings?

A   At the Red Store.

Q   Near what town or school or fort?

A   Near Fort Sill.

Q   Was that hearing place upon the reservation at Fort Sill?

A   Not on the military reservation.

Q   Which direction was it from the reservation and approximately what distance?

A   He orients it by stating that it was east of where the present Indian Mission is located, which would make it about a mile and a half from what is now the Fort Sill railroad station.

Q   And that is southeast of the Fort Sill reservation?

A   Southeast.

Q   Does he remember when he attended the first meeting of the Commission?

A   He doesn't remember that. He first went there the second day of the Council and he just stood around and wasn't there very long and then he went back.

Q   What recognized leaders of the Comanche tribe did he see in attendance the day he was present?

A   Two, Quanah and Ishita. I am not sure of the spelling.

Q   To the best of your memory, how is it spelled?

    INTERPRETER: I-s-h-i-t-a, I think.

Q   He said "Quanah," does he mean Quanah Parker?

A   Yes.

Q   Does he remember the names of any other Comanche chiefs that were there on that day?

A   He doesn't know of any.

Q   Does he remember the names of any white men that were present on that day?

A   No, he does not.

Q   How many white men were there?

A   He said he saw two.

Q   He saw two?

A   Yes, sir.

Q   Did the white men talk to any of the Comanche chiefs there that day?

A   Not while he was there.

Q   Did any one act as an interpreter for the white men there that day?

A   He doesn't know who it was.

Q   Did he attend any other meetings of the Council?

A   No, just that one.

Q   Did he hear Quanah Parker make any statement there on that day?

A   He said he heard Quanah Parker saying that he wanted $2.50 an acre for the land.

Q   Did he hear any one make an explanation as to what the Commission came here for?

A   He said he heard no explanation.

Q   Did he see Lone Wolf at the meeting?

A   White Wolf, you mean?

Q   White Wolf --

A   He doesn't know a person by that name.

Q   Did he see a white woman there that day?

A   He saw a white woman there.

Q   Does he know her name?

A   He doesn't know her name.

Q   Were signatures requested to the Jerome Agreement there that day?

A   He said he saw no one taking signatures the day he was there.

Q   Did he see any one taking signatures at any other time?

A   No.

Q   Does he know what offers were made for the Indian reservation there at this Council meeting?

A   The only thing he heard was Quanah Parker's statement that he wanted $2.50 per acre for the land.

Q   Were there any meetings held by the Comanche tribe later after the meeting?

A   He doesn't know of any.

Q   Was the proposition of Quanah Parkers', of $2.50 an acre, ever submitted to a vote of the members of the Comanche tribe?

A   No.

Q   Did he sign the Jerome Agreement?

A   No.

Q   Could he read and write at that time?

A   No.

Q   Did any member of the Comanche Tribe ask him to sign the agreement?

A   No one asked him.

Q   Does he know that his name appears upon the Jerome Agreement as having signed it?

A   He did not know.

Q   Would he recognize his signature if it was shown to him?

A   He said he would not. He can't write and doesn't read and he would have no way of recognizing his signature.

Q   You may have the witness.

MR. BARNEY: No questions.

WITNESS EXCUSED

CHOCKPAYAH, called on the part of plaintiffs, being first duly sworn, through interpreter Choot, to testify truth, the whole truth and nothing but truth, testified through said interpreter as follows:

(NOTE BY REPORTER: See explanation of reporter heretofore made in this record with reference to questions asked through the interpreter in the third person and answers interpreted in the third person.)

DIRECT EXAMINATION

QUESTIONS BY MR. MISKOVSKY:

Q   What is your name?

A   Chockpayah.

Q   Do you have a given name, or first name?

A   Tom.

Q   Now, is his name spelled other than the way you spelled it in the Comanche language?

INTERPRETER: Well, it could be spelled most any way, since the Comanches depend on whoever writes the name.

MR. MISKOVSKY: Could it be spelled in this manner, Reverend? (Showing witness line 67 of Plaintiffs' Exhibit No. 5, reading "Chok po ya"

A   Yes, sir. (Answer by Interpreter)

MR. MISKOVSKY: Will you spell that into the record?

INTERPRETER: Chok po ya.

Q   Are the first spelling and the second spelling one and the same person?

INTERPRETER: Yes, sir.

Q   Is that correct?

INTERPRETER: That is correct.

Q   What is your age?
A   I am not sure but I think about 83.
Q   What Indian tribe are you a member of?
A   Comanche.
Q   Do you remember the Jerome Commission coming to the Kiowa, Comanche and Apache reservation?
A   Yes, he remembers.
Q   Where did the Commission hold its meetings upon this reservation?
A   At the Red store.
Q   Where was the Red Store located?
A   Near Fort Sill, east of where the Comanche Mission now stands.

Q   Did he attend any of the meetings of the Commission at the Red Store?

A   He was there.

Q   Have him tell us the names of the recognized Comanche chiefs that were present when he was in attendance.

A   He said Quanah Parker was a recognized chief and then there was Iahita and Tabananaca.

Q   How were these chiefs dressed?

A   They were dressed in the regular Indian custom of the time.

Q   Just describe -- Have you described what he said?

A   He says they were dressed in the Indian way of the time.

Q   Were they in full head dress?

A   Quanah Parker was dressed in buckskin and the other chiefs wore blankets and had sort of bracelets around their arms.

Q   Were there any white men present?

A   He said he remembers seeing two white men there. There may have been three, but he says he remembers seeing two.

Q   Does he remember a white woman being present?

A   Yes, there was a white woman.

Q   What was the white woman's name?

A   He says he has forgotten her name.

Q   Who acted as interpreter for the Comanche tribe?

A   A man named Nocktooah.

Q   Was Nocktooah an Indian or a white man?

A   He was white man like you folks.

Q   Does he know what Nocktooah's white-man name was?

A   He says all he knows is that one of his names was Clark. He doesn't know the other name.

Q   And his Indian name was what?

A   He said that is the name given him by the Indians, Nocktooah.

Q   What did the Indian name Nocktooah mean?

A   Protrusions on his ear and because of that that is what they called him - Nocktooah.

Q   And the word "Nocktooah" in Comanche means what?

A   Little Ear, I guess - Baby Ear - Little Ear.

Q   Now, was he present and did he hear any discussions made by Quanah Parker or Tabananaca at the Council meeting the day he attended?

A   He said, as he was there, he saw Tabananaca there and Quanah across there, and they seemed to be in an argument about some matter.

Q   Tell him to continue.

A   He said Tabananaca arose and said to Quanah Parker, he said, "You have had your way long enough. I am going to sell this land for $1.25 an acre."

Q   What did Quanah Parker say he was going to sell the land for?

A   He said Quanah Parker arose and said, addressing the

assemblage, that they were going to sell the land for $2.25 an acre.

Q   Now, did Quanah Parker and Tabananaca remain there or did either one leave after this discussion?

A   They both left.

Q   Now, did he hear any of the Commissioners make any statement as to what the government wanted with the Indians and what the Indians were to receive?

A   No, he said he heard nothing. One man he didn't know by name - he said it was a man with whiskers - he distinctly heard him say that if the Indians were going to be unwilling to sell their land that they would get the land any way, that Washington would have the power and authority to take their lands.

Q   Was that a white man?

A   Yes, sir, a white man.

ANOTHER INDIAN: That needs correction there. He said a man with whiskers told the Indians they would get the land in spite of them, if they refused to agree with them, whether they would receive that or not, and that scared them into agreement of $2.50.

MR. MISKOVSKY: Is that what you understood him to say, Reverend?

INTERPRETER: Not quite all that.

MR. MISKOVSKY: For the benefit of those that are

present here, I wish that you would leave the interpretation of the witness' testimony solely to the interpreter, then at the conclusion of the witness' testimony, if you will contact your lawyers in there are any discrepancies, we will endeavor to recall the witness and have any corrections made that may need to be made.

Q   Did the Commissioners state what the Indians would be paid for the sale of their lands?

A   He said he heard them say that they would receive several army wagon loads -- it would be worth several army wagon loads of money - the price.

Q   Was any figure or amount in round numbers discussed or told that they would receive?

A   No, that was all he heard, that it would be two or three wagon loads of money.

Q   Was it explained that the Indians were to receive land in addition to the money?

A   Yes, he heard them say that the Indians would get land.

Q   How much land were the Indians to receive?

A   He said he heard them say that each male would get what would be the equivalent of two allotments.

Q   Does he know what an allotment consisted of?

A   At that time he did not know.

Q   Was it explained to them how large an area 160 acres was?

A   He said it was measured off and they were shown how

much 160 acres would be.

Q   How was it measured off and how was it shown to them how much 160 acres of land would be?

A   He said they used a chain to measure the area and show them how much it was.

Q   Now, was this staked off in any manner so they could see what that amount of land amounted to?

A   He says that as far as he remembers, they measured one side with a chain and told them that the other side would be the same each direction.

Q   At the time and on the day that he was in attendance were any of the Comanches present asked to sign the Jerome Agreement?

A   No, no one was asked to sign that day and he didn't sign.

Q   Did he return any following day?

A   No, he didn't go back after that one time.

Q   Where did he go after the end of the Council meeting that day?

A   He said he just wandered around the camp.

Q   Did he sign the Jerome Agreement?

A   No, he did not sign.

Q   Did he have any one else sign for him?

A   He gave nobody authority to sign his name.

Q   Can he read or write the English language?

A   No, he cannot read or write.

Q   Can he write his own name in English?

A   No, he can't write. Thumb mark is the only way he signs his name - using his thumb mark.

Q   For the purpose of the record, I direct the witness' attention to Exhibit 5 and particularly to page 4, opposite number 67, and ask you if that is your name which appears opposite that number?

A   He said that he does not know that it is.

Q   Can he sign his name?

A   No.

Q   Would he recognize his signature - I don't mean signature, let me change that. Would he recognize his name if he saw it written?

A   No, he wouldn't.

Q   You may cross examine.

  MR. BARNEY: No questions.

  MR. MISKOVSKY: Does the Commission desire to ask any questions of this witness?

  COMMISSIONER O'MARR: I would like to ask him this question: Did you see any flags there marking the boundaries of 160 acres of land?

A   He says, personally he didn't see a flag. There may have been one, but he didn't see it.

  COMMISSIONER O'MARR: All right.

    WITNESS EXCUSED

(Neda Birdsong called to act as an interpreter and sworn by the clerk to act as such interpreter.)

WAU QUA, called as a witness on the part of plaintiffs, being first duly sworn, through said interpreter, Neda Birdsong, to testify truth, the whole truth and nothing but truth, testified through said interpreter as follows, to-wit:

(NOTE BY REPORTER: See explanation of reporter heretofore made in this record with reference to questions asked through the interpreter in the third person and answers interpreted in the third person.)

DIRECT EXAMINATION

QUESTIONS BY MR. MISKOVSKY:

Q   You may state your name.

A   Wauqua.

Q   Of what Indian tribe are you a member?

A   Comanche.

Q   What is your age?

A   He doesn't know for sure how old he is. He never went to school.

Q   Does he remember the Jerome Commission coming to the Kiowa, Comanche and Apache reservation?

A   Yes.

MR. MISKOVSKY: (To interpreter) Be sure and give all of his answer to the question into the record.

Q   Where did the Commission meet - the Jerome Commission?

A   He said, south of the old Red Store in the hide house.

Q   Now, did he attend any of the meetings of the Jerome Commission?

A   He said that he did not attend a full session, but he went around to this hide house to see what they were doing.

Q   What chiefs of the Comanche tribe were present there?

A   He said, for sure there was Quanah Parker and Tabananaca there.

Q   Now, were any white men present?

A   He said there were three men, he supposed they were white men. He said he didn't pay much mind.

Q   Were there any white women present?

A   He said there was one woman sitting over there in the corner. She had a sunbonnet on.

Q   Who acted as interpreter for the Comanches?

A   He said he didn't know who did the interpreting.

Q   Did he hear any discussions that were had between Quanah Parker and Tabananaca with the Commission?

A   He said, "Here stands Quanah Parker and here stood Tabananaca."

Q   All right, what were they saying?

A   Tabananaca is speaking. Tabananaca says to Quanah Parker, he says, "Now, you look here, I want a dollar and a quarter an acre for this land," and Quanah Parker says to him, he says, "My friend, have pity on me," he says, "I want two dollars and a quarter for all this land."

Q   What else was said?

A   He said that is all he heard and he walked out.

Q   Did he see the signatures being taken there that day to the Jerome Agreement?

A   He said that that woman with the sunbonnet on told him that they were signing their names outside.

Q   Did he sign the Jerome Agreement?

A   No.

Q   Did he ask any one -- (interrupted)

INTERPRETER: Wait a minute. He said he didn't write his name. He can't write his name, nor did he touch the pen and make a "x".

Q   Did he tell any one to sign his name for him to that agreement?

A   No.

Q   Does he know that his name appears upon the Jerome Agreement?

A   No, he doesn't know it.

Q   Now, directing the witness' attention to Plaintiffs' Exhibit 5, and particularly to page 7, I will ask you to direct his attention to the name opposite number 124 and ask him if he recognizes that as his signature and if he wrote that name?

INTERPRETER: He can't write.

MR. MISKOVSKY: Ask him the question, please.

A   No.

Q   Was there any other member of the Comanche tribe - strike that, please. Did he know of any other member of the Comanche tribe with the name of Wauqua?

A   No, in no case, but there was a Weryah, but not a Wauqua.

MR. THOMPSON: Could his name be spelled by syllables phonetically W-o-o-k-w-o-a-h?

INTERPRETER: It is a very difficult thing to do, to ask him that question, since the Comanche is not a written language and they have no conception of spelling.

MR. MISKOVSKY: Do you understand the question, Rev. Choot?

INTERPRETER: Yes, sir, but putting it in Comanche is a very difficult matter.

A   (Interpreting answer of witness) The nearest he could come to it is ask him if there was any other way or any other name that would sound similar to Wauqua, and he says there isn't; that there is no other name that he knows of among the Comanches that could sound like Wauqua.

MR. THOMPSON: Let the record show that we are now speaking of the name appearing opposite number 266 on Exhibit No. 5, spelled "W-o-o-k-w-e-a-h."

Q   Would you ask the witness whether he knows of a Comanche whose name would be pronounced as is number 334, being "W-o-o-k-y-e-y."

A   He says he does not believe it could be his name.

Q   Does he know of an Indian with that name?

A   He says he does not know of any person by that name.

Q   Ask the witness whether he knows, or knew, of an Indian by the name of W-o-o-k-w-e-a-h, being the name opposite number 266 on Exhibit 5.

MR. BARNEY: Your Honors, I feel that I must object to this line of questioning. In the first place, certainly no one has contended that the name opposite 124 is this witness. The government certainly hasn't contended it, but the plaintiffs apparently pick out a name and say "This is not your name?" "This is not you?" and then pick out the name opposite 266 and they say "This isn't you, is it?" No one on the part of the government, at least, has suggested that the name opposite 124 is this witness and no one on the part of the government has suggested that the name opposite number 266 is this witness, and so it is perfectly easy to set these straw men up and then knock them down, but I don't see we are proving anything.

MR. MISKOVSKY: If the Court please, I was under the impression that it was established that the Wauqua, which is the only individual by that name in the tribe, is the signature, or the name, appearing opposite 124, and that is the name of this witness and if there are no other individuals in the tribe by this witness' name, then it must be that this signature that appears opposite 124 is not the signature of this witness, nor was his consent obtained to it, even though it appears there, and that is the purpose of the offer.

COMMISSIONER O'MARR: I think that has been shown here. He has denied that he signed it or that he authorized any one to sign it for him.

MR. BARNEY: There is no testimony that the name "W-o-q-u-a-y" is this witness. Of course he will deny it. He will deny each one on there, but nobody has contended it yet.

MR. THOMPSON: If Your Honors please, you understand that the phonetics involved in this situation is the crux of the issue here.

COMMISSIONER O'MARR: Do you claim that he signed this or that he did not sign it?

MR. THOMPSON: We claim that he did not sign and that his name appears on it.

COMMISSIONER O'MARR: The government does not claim he did sign it.

MR. THOMPSON: I am not sure that the government will never contend that his name is not on this document.

MR. BARNEY: The point is, counsel have picked out a couple of names which they say isn't like the name of this witness and then they put this witness on the stand and say, "Now, this isn't you, is it?" and he says "No."

COMMISSIONER O'MARR: This is clear, he says he did not sign that agreement.

MR. BARNEY: That is all that is necessary, if he didn't sign it, he didn't sign it.

MR. MISKOVSKY: And he says that his name is Wauqua.

COMMISSIONER O'MARR: The name appearing on there might be this man, I don't know, but so far as the record stands now, this man did not sign any agreement. That seems clear to us.

Q (By Mr. Miskovsky) Your name is Wauqua?
A Wauqua.
Q You may cross examine.

CROSS EXAMINATION

QUESTIONS BY MR. BARNEY:

Q How do you spell that?

INTERPRETER: "W-a-u-q-u-a," and I think that is the way it is on his patent.

Q And that is the way his name has been spelled, I believe you said, for fourteen years?

INTERPRETER: Ever since I have known him, yes.

Q How long would that be?

INTERPRETER: I have known him always.

Q Is that the way his name was spelled back in the days of the Jerome Agreement?

INTERPRETER: I think his patent would bear that name.

Q   Well, ask him, is that the way his name was spelled.
A   Yes, he said that in his records at the Agency and his patent, it is all W-a-u-q-u-a.
Q   That is all.

WITNESS EXCUSED

(Joe Niedo called to act as interpreter and duly sworn by the clerk to act as such interpreter.)

MAW WAT, called as a witness on the part of plaintiffs, being first duly sworn, through the interpreter, to testify truth, the whole truth and nothing but truth, testified, through said interpreter, as follows:

(NOTE BY REPORTER: See explanation of reporter heretofore made in this record with reference to questions asked through the interpreter in the third person and answers interpreted in the third person.)

DIRECT EXAMINATION

QUESTIONS BY MR. THOMPSON:
Q   What is your name?
A   Maw wat.
Q   What is your tribe?
A   Comanche.
Q   What does the word "Maw wat" mean in Comanche?
A   He said all he knows, they call him Maw wat, his father, mother and everybody.

Q   What does that word "Maw vat" mean in English?

A   He said that because he hasn't got no hand, that is why they call him "No Hand." "Maw vat" means "No Hand."

(Note by Reporter: The witness, upon answering the question, held up his arm, exhibiting the fact that he had a very small deformed hand on that arm, obviously deformed from birth.)

Q   Can he hear?

INTERPRETER: He can't hear.

MR. THOMPSON: Let the record show that the questions are being put to the witness through the interpreter by the use of sign language.

Q   How old are you?

A   79.

Q   Does he remember when the Jerome Commission came down to deal with the Indians?

A   He said he know, he was there, but he didn't hear what was going on, but he was there.

Q   Did he attend any of the council meetings held by the Jerome Commission?

A   He was there and some of the men told him that they have a meeting upstairs and when they told him a fellow by the name of Marcus Polo, a policeman, told him to stand back, just only six were upstairs to do the business.

Q   Where was that?

A   At the Red Store.

Q   Did he ever go back to another meeting of the Jerome Commission?

A   No.

Q   Did he sign the Jerome Agreement?

A   No, he didn't sign.

Q   Was there another Indian in the Kiowa, Comanche or Apache tribes with a name which, when translated into English, means "No Hand" or Maw wat?

A   No, he is the only one with a name called Maw wat.

Q   Was there any one else with that name?

A   No, he didn't know of any one.

Q   Or a name that when translated into English means "No Hand?"

A   No, he does not know of any one.

MR. THOMPSON: I would invite the Commissioners' attention at this point to the name appearing opposite number 149 on Exhibit 5, and the name appearing opposite 234 on Plaintiffs' Exhibit 5.

Q   You may examine.

CROSS EXAMINATION

QUESTIONS BY MR. BARNEY:

Q   Didn't you spell his name differently a minute ago, M-o-w-a-t? (Speaking to interpreter)

INTERPRETER: Who? Me?

Q   Yes.

A I didn't spell it. (Answer by Interpreter)

Q How do you spell it?

INTERPRETER: I can ask him. Maybe he has got a record. I don't know how to spell it. Maybe he has got the record.

Q Will you pronounce the name in English as nearly as you can translate it from Comanche? I want to get the sound, is what I am after.

INTERPRETER: No Hand.

Q That is the English, what is the Comanche?

A Maw wat. (By Interpreter)

Q Maw wat?

A Yes. (By Interpreter)

Q Now, if you were going to write that in English, how would you write Maw wat?

INTERPRETER: I don't have much education, I don't know how to pronounce it. I wouldn't know how. You see, you and him might not spell it the same way. When you hear it, maybe you get it "My-" and maybe he get it "Mz--" I say, maybe he got the record. They got to spell according to the sound, how a man catches it.

Q And you understand his Comanche name to sound in English like "Maw wat", is that right, or am I wrong?

A INTERPRETER: Maw-a-wat. No Hand, Maw-a-wat.

Q Maw-a-wat.

INTERPRETER: You see, there is a sound right in

between.

Q   In other words, you could say there were three syllables to it, Maw-a-wat?

A   Maw-a-wat. (By interpreter)

Q   And you wouldn't know who to spell that for us?

INTERPRETER: No, I won't.

Q   That is all.

WITNESS EXCUSED

TENNYSON BERRY, called as a witness on the part of plaintiffs, being first duly sworn to testify truth, the whole truth and nothing but truth, testified as follows:

DIRECT EXAMINATION

QUESTIONS BY MR. THOMPSON:

Q   Will you state your name.

A   Tennyson Berry, member of Kiowa-Apache.

Q   How old are you?

A   69.

Q   Did you attend any of the meetings of the Jerome Commission?

A   No, sir.

Q   At the time that the Jerome Commission came to Fort Sill and Anadarko would you tell us who the Apache chiefs were?

A   Whiteman, or Sa cha to klanie.

Q   Were there other Apache chiefs?

A   Yes, sir. Che waeth lanie.

Q   What does that mean when translated into English?

A   That means a whole lot of trees or timber.

Q   Were there any other Apache chiefs?

A   No, two.

Q   I show you page 25 of Plaintiffs' Exhibit 5, and direct your attention to 412 and the name appearing opposite that A-chil-tah, and ask you what that means translated into English?

A   That means "All of it."

Q   All of it?

A   All of it.

Q   I show you page 27 of Plaintiffs' Exhibit 5, and direct your attention to the name appearing opposite the number 451, Ah-chil-ty, and ask you what that means when translated into English?

A   That would mean the same thing.

Q   I will ask you, from your knowledge of the Apache language, are these two names the same names?

A   Yes, sir.

Q   Were there two individuals in the tribe with this same name?

A   No, sir.

Q   Is this an Apache name?
A   Yes, sir.
Q   Do you know the Indian called A-chil-tah?
A   Yes, sir.
Q   Do you know whether he signed the Jerome Agreement?
A   No, sir.
Q   Are any of the old chiefs you mentioned still alive?
A   No, sir.
Q   Have you examined the purported signatures to the Jerome Agreement to see whether any of the individuals appearing on here by name as members of the Apache tribe are alive?
A   No, sir.
Q   You mean by that that there are none of the Apaches alive?
A   No one alive.
Q   You say no one?
A   All gone.
Q   To the Happy Hunting Ground?
A   Yes, sir.
Q   Will you tell the court here what you remember about the Jerome Commission and what happened during and after their visit down here?
A   Well, I was in school at the time, 1892, in Kiowa school right close to Anadarko, and I heard about this Jerome treaty with our people here and so at that time it looked

like, you know, the Kiowa, Comanche and Apache tribes - it looked like they all separated. First, you know, they wanted to make a grass lease or sell grass land, and part of them don't want to sell grass at all and some of them wanted to, and that is the way it went, and so when this treaty come, it was just the same way. Of course, I know, the Apaches living over there where Cement is now, they all didn't want to sell grass, and so when this treaty come over here - the Commissioners come - they still were mad and so there was very few Apaches here, I understand. And about 1898 I was at Carlile and a delegation came from Quanah Parker's boys, for me to go to Washington to meet these chiefs. All right, we went. We got to Washington. All right, we went to Washington - got to Washington, and the next day we see Commissioner of Indian Affairs. I think his name was Morgan, or Jones. I am kinda mixed - I don't know which one - long time ago. All right, when we went into the Commissioner's office, the Commissioner got up from his seat and made Quanah Parker put his arms around him - love him so much. All right, then we was sitting there. Quanah Parker was telling the Commissioner, "I come long ways. I want to tell you, my people down there don't want to sell no land. They want to keep it, all the time, which I am using that way of living." Commissioner told him, "Quanah, I told you and the other chiefs that as long as I am the Commissioner of Indian Affairs, your land never will be sold. You are going to stay right there just like it is for a long time." That is what he told Quanah Parker and the other chiefs, but it wasn't two years after that, in June 1900, here comes Congress and passes a law that this country must be opened and did open it. What the Commissioner told Quanah, I guess he couldn't help himself, I don't know. That is as much as I know about it.

Q   No further questions.

CROSS EXAMINATION

QUESTIONS BY MR. BARNEY:

Q   You say some of the Indians didn't want to sell grass and others did want to sell grass?

A   Yes, sir.

Q   Some of the Indians didn't want to sell the land and others did want to sell the land, is that right?

A   Yes, sir.

Q   And the Indians just didn't agree among themselves as to whether the surplus lands should be sold or held, is that right?

A   According to the Apaches - I am talking about Kiowa-Apaches, I am not talking about Comanches - I am speaking what I hear - that then the Apache chief says: "You Comanches get together, but I am just going to stay right in between you. If you get together, I am going to go with you, if not, I am going to stay right here." That is what the Apache chief says.

Q Do you know from hearing your father and other people talk what the Comanches wanted to do? Did they want to sell the land or did they want to hold the land?

A I don't think they wanted to sell very bad from the start.

Q Which did the Kiowas want to do?

A The Kiowas are worse - they say they don't want to sell it at all.

Q Your father said that he wanted the Comanches and Kiowas to get together, what did he mean by that? What were they at odds about?

A If they want to sell the lands it is all right. If not, they would both stick together, but they never did as far as I heard.

Q Perhaps I don't understand you. Some of the Indians wanted to sell and some of them didn't, and your father said "When you get together among yourselves, then I will join with you," is that right?

A Yes, sir.

Q That is all.

WITNESS EXCUSED

ALBERT ATTOCKNIE, called as a witness by plaintiffs, being first duly sworn to testify truth, the whole truth and nothing but truth testified (without interpreter) as follows, to-wit:

DIRECT EXAMINATION

QUESTIONS BY MR. THOMPSON:

Q   What is your name?

A   Albert Attocknie. White man would say Lone Teacher.

Q   What is your tribe?

A   Commanche.

Q   How old are you?

A   I was on the Agency records, shown to be born in 1880.

Q   Did you go to school?

A   I went to government school at the same time as my friend Tennyson Berry,

Q   How long did you go to school?

A   About three years, maybe four.

Q   Did you attend any of the meetings of the Jerome Commission here with the older members of your family?

A   I did not, except to just go to the meeting and back. I never attended as a listener.

Q   But you went to the meeting place?

A   Every day, it seemed like.

Q   Do you remember any of the discussions that took place

after the members of your family had returned to your place of residence, after the meetings?

A   Yes, sir

Q   Would you tell us what the general nature of those discussions were?

A   Fifty-eight years ago is a long ways back for memory. I remember though one time a big white man and a white woman, I don't remember her name now, came to our camp at our council meeting, but at our camp.

Q   Do you remember the white man's name?

A   No, he was a very large man and had whiskers.

Q   Was he one of the Commissioners?

A   I do not know.

Q   All right, proceed.

A   And he called my people to a meeting. Now, this is not at the Jerome council meeting; this is at our camp. We were camped about a mile north of the Jerome council meeting, and I remember him telling, the Commissioner, telling those gathered there that if they did not sell their land, nor agree to sell their land, Washington would take their land away from them for nothing. I heard the interpreter say that.

Q   Who was the interpreter?

A   I do not know her name - white woman.

Q   Was it Emsy S. Smith?

A   It might be. I don't know.

Q   And then what happened on that occasion?

A   I don't know. I just got scared. I thought Washington was going to jerk our land from under us, and I got scared, and that is all.

Q   What members of your family were present on that occasion?

A   My father was there, and my uncle - my mother's brother, Cheevers, was there, and Tabananca was there.

Q   Do you remember any one else there?

A   And Howeah was there.

Q   Spell that.

A   I have just a second grade education.

Q   H-o-w-e-a-h?

A   I would guess. And they were discussing about the price they were going to get for it and none of the old Indians seemed to know how much it was. I did hear two million dollars mentioned, either by the white man or the interpreter. I don't remember that. But no one asked to see how much that it prorated among the people of the tribes. I know they don't know what they were talking about, although, as one of the witnesses said, there was a plot measured off, and one of the witnesses said my brother, now deceased, help pull a chain along to show how much a quarter section was, and I helped put up one corner.

Q   Did you put poles up?

A   I drug a pole and my brother dug a hole in the ground and set up the pole, and tied a rag on top, and there were four floating around at each corner, but they didn't know how much one acre was, and a lot of us don't know how much land measures an acre. I remember doing horse racing at that time with a few white people. If one Indian wants to have a race with a white man - to give you an idea how they understood how much an acre is - they go to challenge to a horse race and the Indian says "How many acres we run?" for the measurement the horses are going to run. Now, that is the idea he has. Your horse and my horse is going to run, now, how many acres?" That is the idea we had at that time.

Q Now, you mentioned that there were certain of your relatives at this conference?

A Yes, sir.

Q At which time the statement was made that the land would be taken away from the Indians whether they signed or not, is that correct?

A That is correct.

Q Now, which of your relatives that you mentioned, giving us their names, signed the Jerome Agreement?

A I do not know other than what I see on the paper now.

Q What are those names you see on the paper now?

A I see my father was a signer, number 17.

Q And what was his name?

A Attocknie, the same name I bear now.

Q   All right, were there others?

A   I see my brother signed his name. I do not remember how it is spelled there. I remember Tahkay is the way we spelled it.

Q   Would that be number 18, Tahpony?

A   No, that is another old man. That man's name is pronounced Tah-pon-y. His name is Tahpony.

Q   Well, are there any others?

A   That signed the treaty?

Q   Whose names you have observed on the Agreement that were present on this occasion on which the statement was made which you testified to.

A   That is all I remember just off-hand now.

Q   From your listening to the conversation that occurred around other camp fires after the meeting, can you tell us what the general opinion was among the Indians as to how much per acre the tribes were getting for their surplus lands?

A   I do not know. This meeting I have particularly in mind, when I got scared about Washington taking the land away from us, was held in the morning before the general council meeting at the treaty. It was early in the morning when he come there with this white woman interpreter in a buggy.

Q   Well, do you know how much the Indians expected to get

per acre for their land? What was the accepted figure?

A   I do not know. I don't remember; but something they didn't know anything about. Even now we don't know how much land measure an acre is. I doubt very much if any of these older men like me know how much an acre would measure off.

Q   Did you know, or did the Indians at that time know what two millions dollars was?

A   No.

Q   Do Indians now know how much two million dollars is?

A   I doubt that very much. I don't know. I might write it down, but I wouldn't know how much it is.

Q   Is there anything else you would like to tell the Commission of your knowledge respecting the Jerome Agreement and the negotiations and what took place afterwards?

A   No, that was all. I just want to show the Commission that the Indians didn't know what they were doing. They didn't know how much land they had to sell and they didn't know how much the land would prorate among them. Nobody asked that.

CROSS EXAMINATION

QUESTIONS BY MR. BARNEY:

Q   How many acres did your horse run that day, Albert?

A   What is it?

Q   How many acres did your horse run that day?

A   How many acres? I do not know.

Q   Well, did he win?

A   I don't remember which one won.

Q   You said that you went to the council meetings with your parents and it seemed like you went every day.

A   It seems like, as near as I can remember, I went every day and maybe two or three times a day.

Q   And for how many days?

A   At least two days.

Q   At least two days?

A   Yes, sir.

Q   Did they hold meetings in the morning and then quit and then come back in the afternoon?

A   It seems to me like that I let my father off at the meeting and would go back for him at noon and by that I believe they must have had meetings in the forenoon.

Q   Would they have any at night, that is, after sundown?

A   I do not remember.

Q   Albert, were these councils pretty well attended by the Indians? Were there lots of Indians in attendance at the councils - the various meetings?

A   It seems like when somebody mentioned Tabananaca, at that time it just seems like I saw that white man standing up and there was a crowd, I believe bigger than the crowd in here and it seems like they were all sitting down on the ground, most of the Indians, and the white people were sitting up higher and our chiefs sat higher up, it seems to me like. I don't think they had many chairs.

Q   But the Indians, as you saw them there, were there listening to what was going on?

A   It seemed like that, yes, sir.

Q   I realize it is hard to remember fifty-eight years ago, that is a hard thing to do.

A   Especially when one gets old. You are getting there.

Q   I am getting there. I have got almost as many grey hairs as you have.   What did Tabananaca say? What did he want?

A   I do not remember on which side he was on.

Q   There were two sides, weren't there?

A   What is it?

Q   There were two sides? Some of the Indians were on one side and some were on the other side?

A   I don't know. I just heard the two sides from Tennyson Berry, just in this council room now.

Q   I see. All right. You do remember hearing the two million dollars mentioned?

A   Yes, sir, it seems like I remember those figures.

Q   And that was mentioned in connection with what the Indians were going to get for the lands which they sold to the government, is that the way you remember it?

A   The way I remember it, that is the offer. I don't say that the Indians were willing to take it, but it seems like I remember the white woman interpreter say that, and I know she was trying to explain how much two million dollars was and my friend here already stated it would be a wagon load of money.

Q   Did the Comanche Indians ever get paid in boxes of money, Albert?

A   I don't remember seeing one, but I heard silver money comes in boxes.

Q   If I was to say to you that I was going to pay you a box of money, how much would you understand I meant?

A   I don't know now. Since white man has mentioned this thing, I would be very sceptical about what it is, from my experience now.

Q   Well, let's assume that I am honest. Wasn't that supposed to be one thousand dollars in the old days?

A   I think I heard somebody say that, since we got to talking about this lawsuit.

Q   I understand you were just a young boy then?

A   I was just a boy, yes. I thought I was a big man but I wasn't. I got scared, you know, when I thought they were going to take the land away from us - I got scared.

Q   I think that is all.

WITNESS EXCUSED

MR. THOMPSON: May it please the Court, at this time I would like to read into the record a short extract from a book entitled "Some Memories of a Soldier," by Hugh Lenox Scott, Major General, United States Army, Retired; published by the Century Company, copyrighted "1928," I read from the volume which is in the repository in the Library of Congress, and at page 199. Before I read the extract, I would like, by way of introduction, to state that these remarks by Major General Scott are remarks by the same Hugh L. Scott, or H. L. Scott, who was identified as being the Commanding Officer of Troop "L", Seventh Calvary, which was a troop stationed at Fort Sill and composed entirely of Indians from this reservation. I also invite the Court's attention to the fact that in Section 10 of the Jerome Agreement, as originally signed but not as adopted by Congress, Hugh L. Scott appears as a beneficiary of an allotment of this land if the Jerome Agreement is ratified. I state that to indicate that General Scott stood to benefit by the ratification of the Jerome Agreement. This is what General Scott says:

"In 1892 the Cherokee Commission came to the Indian Territory to arrange for the purchase of the Indian lands for settlement by white people. Its members were charged with all sorts of irregularities in obtaining agreements. The Kiowas, Comanches, and Kiowa Apaches elected me to take a delegation of their tribes to Washington to prevent the ratification of the treaty by Congress. Some of the influential Indians were said to have sold out the interests of their people to the Cherokee Commission. Quanah Parker, chief of the Comanches, was in favor of ratification. He got permission to visit his children at Carlisle and ran over to Washington without the knowledge of his agent, and arranged for a hearing before the Committee on Indian Affairs, of which Mr. Holman of Indiana, often referred to as the Watch-Dog of the Treasury, was chairman.

Quanah's appointment for a hearing was on the day we arrived in Washington, and my delegation attended the hearing. It was Quanah's appointment, and he had it all his own way at first, and held the sympathy of the committee, who wanted to open the land for settlement by the white man. The committee was about to close the hearing and go to lunch when I asked for my day in court. The chairman asked, "Who are you, and what are you, a white man, doing here?" I handed him my card, and he exclaimed, "Why, you are a soldier; how do you come here?" I told him I was there by order of the commanding general of the army. Quanah jumped up in great rage and said he wouldn't have any white man speak for him or his people.

I said: "Quanah objects to my speaking here for the Kiowa and Comanche people, but he is speaking only for himself and not for his people, who have not sent him here, and he does not represent their sentiment. If he has any credentials, as I know he has not, let him produce them. Here are my credentials, signed by the agent of the Kiowa and Comanche people, certifying to my election with this delegation to represent them in open council, and I would like to be heard." Whereupon the committee agreed to hear me for an hour at 1:00 P.M.

We met and quarreled from 1:00 until 5:00 P.M., the delegate from Oklahoma the most conspicuous in the opposition in support of Quanah. We metaphorically kicked shins, pulled hair, gouged, bit, and scratched, catch-as-catch-can, no holds barred, all the afternoon. Quanah announced his intention of killing me before I could get back to Fort Sill, and the committee reserved decision.

The Southwest from St. Louis down was determined to open the country, fraud or no fraud. In those days I used to be the enemy of the Indian Department and everybody in it, but three men I knew to be honest, James McLaughlin, J. George Wright, and Major Larrabee in the Indian Office; and I set out to arrange an interview with President Cleveland through the War Department. I knew nothing of the tangled mazes in those days to be found in Washington--wheels within wheels, and deep pits for simple people like me--but some of the wiser men in the War Department advised me to arrange my interview through the Commissioner of Indian Affairs, Mr. Browning.

Ahpiatom, a Kiowa of my delegation, made a great impression among the senators and congressmen in the President's anteroom. He was beautifully dressed in soft yellow buckskin with long fringes, and with his silver medal on his breast. He looked off down the Potomac like an eagle off a crag, paying no more attention to the senators handling his ornaments than if they had been ants crawling about his feet, and despising their effeminate curiosity about his trinkets.

We went in with Commissioner Browning, and when I had finished stating my case to the President he jumped up from behind his desk, striking one hand into the other in emphatic indignation, and exclaimed: "I will not permit it. I will see justice done to those Indians as long as I'm in power!" And he did. Through the influence of President Cleveland and of Senator Matt Quay of Pennsylvania, who had a romantic interest in the Indian as well as a wide knowledge of them and their history that filled me with amazement, the ratification of that agreement was prevented, against all the power of the Southwest, for seven years; but I later picked up a newspaper in Havana and read that it had been ratified, fraud and all."

MR. THOMPSON: Now, may it please the Court, we have no Indian witnesses present this evening. We expected to have about four or five in the morning. However, we have some documentary evidence that we can start in and introduce in the record. It has been discussed, for the most part, with Government counsel and we can get that by us this evening, if the Commission is so desirous.

COMMISSIONER O'MARR: We just as well proceed with that.

MR. THOMPSON: We offer, as the Plaintiffs' Exhibit No. 13, Senate Executive Document 17, 52nd Congress, 2nd Session, being the message from the President of the United States transmitting to the Senate and the House of Representatives, the Jerome Agreement. This exhibit contains a letter from the Secretary of the Interior; a report from the Commissioner of Indian Affairs, T. J. Morgan; a letter signed by David H. Jerome and Warren G. Sayre, who were two of the commissioners; a letter by the Assistant Attorney General, and the transmittal letter signed by all of the Commissioners; and ask that it be received in evidence as Plaintiffs' Exhibit No. 13.

MR. BARNEY: No objection.

COMMISSIONER O'MARR: It may be received.

(The said exhibit, Plaintiffs' Exhibit No. 13, admitted in evidence as above shown, is included in the "Book of Exhibit at page number 17 thereof.)

COMMISSIONER O'MARR: What about the preceding exhibit? There has been no ruling on that. Are there any objections to it?

MR. BARNEY: That wasn't offered as an exhibit. That

was read into the record, Your Honor.

MR. THOMPSON: If the Commission would prefer, for convenience, I have an extract from it.

COMMISSIONER O'MARR: No, we would prefer to have it in the record.

MR. THOMPSON: As, of course, was to be anticipated, the Congressional machinery started turning on the President's Message and I next offer in evidence, as the Plaintiffs' Exhibit 14, a Bill, Senate 3714, to ratify and confirm this agreement - I don't give the full title - the 52nd Congress, 2nd Session, which was introduced on January 13, 1893, by Mr. Dawes.

MR. BARNEY: No objection.

COMMISSIONER O'MARR: It may be received.

(The said exhibit, Plaintiffs' Exhibit No. 14, admitted in evidence as above shown, is included in the "Book of Exhibits," at page number 18 thereof.)

MR. THOMPSON: I next offer in evidence, as Plaintiffs' Exhibit 15, a House Bill, H. R. 10213, the same Congress, introduced by Mr. Harvey, being a bill to ratify and confirm this agreement.

MR. BARNEY: No objection.

COMMISSIONER O'MARR: It may be received.

(The said exhibit, Plaintiffs' Exhibit No. 15, admitted in evidence as above shown, is included in the "Book of Exhibits" at page number 19 thereof.)

MR. THOMPSON: I next offer in evidence, as the Plaintiffs' Exhibit No. 16, a Bill in the House of Representatives, being H. R. 2877, 53d Congress, 1st Session, introduced by Mr. Flynn on September 14, 1893, and ask that it be admitted in evidence as the plaintiffs' next exhibit.

MR. BARNEY: No objection.

COMMISSIONER O'MARR: It may be received.

(The said Exhibit, Plaintiffs' Exhibit No. 16, admitted in evidence as shown above, is included in the "Book of Exhibits" at page number 20 thereof.)

MR. THOMPSON: I next offer in evidence, as the Plaintiffs' Exhibit No. 17, H. R. 4456, introduced in the House of Representatives, 53d Congress, 2d Session, by Mr. Cockrell, on December 5, 1893, being a Bill to ratify and confirm the Jerome Agreement.

MR. BARNEY: No objection.

COMMISSIONER O'MARR: It may be received.

(The said Exhibit, Plaintiffs' Exhibit No. 17, admitted in evidence as shown above, is included in the "Book of Exhibits," forming a part of this transcript, at page number 21 thereof.)

MR. THOMPSON: I next offer in evidence, as the Plaintiffs' Exhibit No. 18, Senate Miscellanous Document No. 102, 53d Congress, 2nd Session, being the official print of a Memoral which was published by the Senate, introduced March 1, 1894, being a protest, together with certain accompanying letters of protest, signed by the Indians - purportedly signed by 324 of the Indians, against the Jerome Agreement, and ask it be received in evidence as the Plaintiffs' Exhibit 18.

MR. BARNEY: No objection.

COMMISSIONER O'MARR: It may be received.

The said Exhibit, Plaintiffs' Exhibit No. 18, admitted in evidence, is included in the "Book of Exhibits," comprising a part of this transcript, at page number 22 thereof.)

MR. THOMPSON: I next offer in evidence, as the Plaintiffs' Exhibit No. 19, Senate Bill 1586, 53rd Congress, 2nd Session, being introduced by Mr. Jones of Arkansas, February 8, 1894, being a bill to ratify and confirm this agreement.

MR. BARNEY: No objection.

COMMISSIONER O'MARR: It may be received.

(The said Exhibit, Plaintiffs' Exhibit No. 19, admitted in evidence, is included in the "Book of Exhibits" forming a part of this transcript, at page number 23 thereof.)

BY MR. THOMPSON: I next offer in evidence, as the Plaintiffs' Exhibit No. 20, H. R. 2877, 53d Congress, 3rd Session, as that bill was reported from the Committee on Indian Affairs February 6, 1895, and ask that it be admitted in evidence.

MR. BARNEY: No objection.

COMMISSIONER O'MARR: It may be received.

(The said Exhibit, Plaintiffs' Exhibit No. 20, is included in the "Book of Exhibits," comprising a part of this transcript, at page numbered 24 thereof.)

MR. THOMPSON: I next offer in evidence, as the Plaintiffs' Exhibit No. 21, the accompanying House Report, being House Report No. 1775, of the same Congress, being presented by Mr. Maddox on February 6, 1895. I make the offer at this time.

MR. BARNEY: No objection.

COMMISSIONER O'MARR: It may be received.

(The said Exhibit, Plaintiffs' Exhibit No. 21, is included in the "Book of Exhibits," forming a part of this transcript, at page numbered 25 thereof.)

MR. THOMPSON: I next offer in evidence, as the Plaintiffs' Exhibit No. 22, H. R. 1468, 54th Congress, 1st Session, being introduced by Mr. Flynn on December 12, 1895, and ask that it be received in evidence.

MR. BARNEY: No objection.

COMMISSIONER O'MARR: It may be received.

(The said Exhibit, Plaintiffs' Exhibit No. 22, admitted in evidence, is included in the "Book of Exhibits," comprising a part of this transcript, at page number 26 thereof.)

MR. THOMPSON: I offer in evidence, as the Plaintiffs' Exhibit No. 23, H. R. Bill 5111, 54th Congress, 1st Session, being a bill to ratify and confirm this Agreement, introduced by Mr. Cockrell, January 29, 1896.

MR. BARNEY: No objection

COMMISSIONER O'MARR: It may be received.

(The said Exhibit, Plaintiffs' Exhibit No. 22, admitted in evidence, is included in the "Book of Exhibits" comprising a part of this transcript, at page number 27 thereof.)

MR. THOMPSON: I offer in evidence, as Plaintiffs' Exhibit No. 24, H. R. 2917, 55th Congress, 1st Session, being a bill in the House of Representatives by Mr. Stephens, on April 21, 1897, being a bill to ratify and confirm this agreement.

MR. BARNEY: No objection.

COMMISSIONER O'MARR: It will be received.

(The said Exhibit, Plaintiffs' Exhibit No. 24, admitted in evidence, is included in the "Book of Exhibits" comprising a part of this transcript, at page number 28 thereof.)

MR. THOMPSON: I offer next in evidence, as Plaintiffs' Exhibit No. 25, H. R. 2917, 55th Congress, 2nd Session, as that bill is reported from the House Indian Affairs Committee on February 10, 1898.

MR. BARNEY: No objection.

COMMISSIONER O'MARR: It may be received.

(The said Exhibit, Plaintiffs' Exhibit No. 25, admitted in evidence, is included in the "Book of Exhibits" comprising a part of this transcript, at page number 29 thereof.)

MR. THOMPSON: I offer in evidence, as Plaintiffs' Exhibit No. 26, the accompanying Report, in the House of Representatives, being House Report No. 431, 55th Congress, 2nd Session, to accompany H. R. 2917, the last exhibit, being a print dated February 10, 1898.

MR. BARNEY: No objection.

COMMISSIONER O'MARR: It may be received.

(The said Exhibit, Plaintiffs' Exhibit No. 26, admitted in evidence, is included in the "Book of Exhibits" comprising a part of this transcript, at page number 30 thereof.)

MR. THOMPSON: I offer in evidence, as Plaintiffs' Exhibit No. 27, H. R. 10049, 55th Congress, 2nd Session, introduced by Mr. Stephens on April 22, 1898, being a bill to ratify and confirm the Jerome Agreement.

MR. BARNEY: No objection.

COMMISSIONER O'MARR: Let it be received.

(The said Exhibit, Plaintiffs' Exhibit No. 27, admitted in evidence, is included in the "Book of Exhibits" comprising a part of this transcript, at page number 31 thereof.)

MR. THOMPSON: I offer in evidence, as Plaintiffs' Exhibit No. 28, H. R. 10049, 55th Congress, 2nd Session, as reported --

MR. BARNEY: No objection.

MR. THOMPSON: Wait a minute. Strike "as reported." --being the print of the bill as it appeared on the House floor.

MR. BARNEY: No objection.

COMMISSIONER O'MARR: It will be received.

(The said Exhibit, Plaintiffs' Exhibit No. 28, admitted in evidence, is included in the "Book of Exhibits" comprising a part of this transcript, at page number 32 thereof.)

MR. THOMPSON: I offer in evidence, as Plaintiffs' Exhibit 29, the accompanying House Report to the preceding exhibit, being House Report No. 1281, 55th Congress, 2nd Session, under date of May 9, 1898, being report by Mr. Curtis of Kansas.

MR. BARNEY: No objection.

COMMISSIONER O'MARR: It may be received.

(The said Exhibit, Plaintiffs' Exhibit No. 29, admitted in evidence, is included in the "Book of Exhibits" comprising a part of this transcript, at page number 33 thereof.)

MR. THOMPSON: I offer in evidence, as Plaintiffs' Exhibit No. 30, H. R. 10049, 55th Congress, 2nd Session, as that bill appeared in the Senate of the United States, after having passed the House of Representatives, dated May 17, 1898.

MR. BARNEY: No objection.

COMMISSIONER O'MARR: It may be received.

(The said Exhibit, Plaintiffs' Exhibit No. 30, admitted in evidence, is included in the "Book of Exhibits" comprising a part of this transcript, at page number 34 thereof.)

MR. THOMPSON: I offer in evidence, as Plaintiffs' Exhibit No. 31, an Amendment to H. R. 10049, intended to be proposed by Mr. Chilton, in the Senate of the United States, dated January 7, 1899.

MR. BARNEY: No objection.

COMMISSIONER O'MARR: It may be received.

(The said exhibit, Plaintiffs' Exhibit No. 31, admitted in evidence, is included in the "Book of Exhibits" comprising a part of this transcript, at page number 35 thereof.)

MR. THOMPSON: I offer in evidence, as Plaintiffs' Exhibit No. 32, Senate Document No. 84, 55th Congress, 3rd Session, being a letter from the Secretary of the Interior in response to a Resolution of the Senate respecting the number of adult male Indians belonging to the Kiowa, Comanche and Apache tribes in October, 1892, being a document dated January 28, 1899.

MR. BARNEY: No objection.

COMMISSIONER O'MARR: It may be received.

(The said exhibit, Plaintiffs' Exhibit No. 32, admitted in evidence, is included in the "Book of Exhibits" comprising a part of this transcript, at page number 36 thereof.)

MR. THOMPSON: I offer in evidence, as Plaintiffs' Exhibit No. 33, H. R. 10049, 55th Congress, 3rd Session, being the print of the bill in the Senate of the United

States, as reported by Mr. Jones of Arkansas, from the Senate Indian Affairs Committee, being dated February 9, 1899.

MR. BARNEY: No objection.

COMMISSIONER O'MARR: It may be admitted.

(The said exhibit, Plaintiffs' Exhibit No. 33, admitted in evidence, is included in "Book of Exhibits" comprising a part of this transcript, at page number 37 thereof.)

MR. THOMPSON: I offer in evidence as Plaintiffs' Exhibit 34, H. R. 905, 56th Congress, 1st Session, being a bill to ratify and confirm the Jerome Agreement, introduced by Mr. Stephens on December 5, 1899.

MR. BARNEY: No objection.

COMMISSIONER O'MARR: It may be received.

(The said exhibit, Plaintiffs' Exhibit No. 34, admitted in evidence, is included in the "Book of Exhibits" comprising a part of this transcript, at page number 38 thereof.)

MR. THOMPSON: I offer, as Plaintiffs' Exhibit No. 35, Senate 255, 56 Congress, 1st Session, being a bill introduced by Mr. Shoup of December 6, 1899, in the Senate, this being a bill to ratify an agreement with the Indians of the Fort Hall Indian reservation in Idaho, and making appropriations to carry the same into effect. I can appreciate that the Commissioners will ask what relevancy that could have to this case. It is just this, may it please the Commission, the Jerome Agreement, as finally enacted with amendments, was Section 6 of the Act which I have quoted from, S. 255, the original bill of which is offered as evidence at this time.

MR. BARNEY: No objection.

COMMISSIONER O'MARR: It may be received.

(The said exhibit, Plaintiffs' Exhibit No. 35, admitted in evidence, is included in the "Book of Exhibits" comprising a part of this transcript, at page number 39 thereof.)

MR. THOMPSON: I offer as the Plaintiffs' Exhibit No. 36, Senate 1352, 56th Congress, 1st Session, being a bill to ratify and confirm an agreement with the Comanche, Kiowa and Apache Indians, introduced by Mr. Chilton on December 11, 1899.

MR. BARNEY: No objection.

COMMISSIONER O'MARR: It may be received.

(The said exhibit, Plaintiffs' Exhibit No. 36, admitted in evidence, is included in the "Book of Exhibits" comprising a part of this transcript, at page number 40 thereof.)

MR. THOMPSON: I next offer in evidence, as Plaintiffs' Exhibit No. 37, Senate 255, 56th Congress, 1st Session, being the bill to ratify the Fort Hall Indian treaty as peported from the Senate Indian Affairs Committee by Mr. Shoup, under date of January 11, 1900.

MR. BARNEY: No objection.

COMMISSIONER O'MARR: It may be received.

(The said exhibit, Plaintiffs' Exhibit No. 37, admitted in evidence, is included in the "Book of Exhibits" comprising a part of this transcript, at page number 41 thereof.)

MR. THOMPSON: I next offer in evidence, as Plaintiffs' Exhibit No. 38, H. R. 5024, 56th Congress, 1st Session, being a bill in the House of Representatives, introduced by Mr. Flynn, to ratify and confirm the Jerome Agreement.

MR. BARNEY: No objection.

COMMISSIONER O'MARR: It will be received.

(The said exhibit, Plaintiffs' Exhibit No. 38, admitted in evidence, is included in the "Book of Exhibits" comprising a part of this transcript, at page number 42 thereof.)

MR. THOMPSON: I might state that I have been reciting "Jerome Agreement" rather than giving the full title as it appears in the bills.

MR. THOMPSON: I next offer in evidence, as Plaintiff's Exhibit No. 39, Senate Document No. 75, 56th Congress,

1st Session, being a letter from the Secretary of the Interior, transmitting Response to Resolution of the Senate, concerning the quantity, nature, and character of the lands of the Kiowa, Comanche, and Apache reservation; the document being dated January 15, 1900.

MR. BARNEY: Just a minute as to that. To that portion of the exhibit which are official communications, the defendant makes no objection; however, the defendant does desire to object to certain statements, commencing on Page 9 of the exhibit, which are merely affidavits made by various persons and which are included as a part of the Senate report. Now, Your Honors, I realize that we don't want to take the time to argue that question here. However, I would like, upon returning to Washington, to submit to the Commission a very short brief on the matter. There have been some decided cases by the Court of Claims and I would like to call those to the attention of the Commission before a ruling is made. Of course, I will supply a copy of the brief on the matter to counsel for the plaintiffs, but I would like for Your Honors to reserve the ruling until I have an opportunity to present the objection.

COMMISSIONER O'MARR: The ruling will be reserved until a later day.

(The said exhibit, Plaintiffs' Exhibit No. 39, to which objection was made and ruling reserved, is included in the "Book of Exhibits" comprising a part of this transcript, at page number 43 thereof.)

MR. THOMPSON: I offer in evidence, as Plaintiffs' Exhibit No. 40, Senate Document No. 76, 56th Congress, 1st Session, being a Memorial from the Kiowa, Comanche, and Apache Indian tribes, dated January 13, 1900, opposing the ratification of the Jerome Agreement; the document being dated January 15, 1900.

MR. BARNEY: No objection.

COMMISSIONER O'MARR: It may be received.

(The said exhibit, Plaintiffs' Exhibit No. 40, admitted in evidence, is included in Book of Exhibits, comprising a part of this transcript, at page number 44 thereof.)

MR. THOMPSON: I offer, as Plaintiffs' Exhibit No. 41, a copy, taken from the National Archives, of a letter addressed to The Honorable, The Secretary of the Interior, signed by W. A. Jones, Commissioner, dated January 19, 1900, referring to the protests, one of which we discussed early this morning, which was not forwarded until 1900, this being a communication taken from the official records of the United States.

MR. BARNEY: No objection.

COMMISSIONER O'MARR: It may be received.

(The said exhibit, Plaintiffs' Exhibit No. 41, admitted in evidence, is included in the "Book of Exhibits" comprising a part of this transcript, at page number 45 thereof.)

MR. THOMPSON: I offer in evidence, as Plaintiffs' Exhibit No. 42, House Document No. 333, 56th Congress, 1st Session, being a Memorial from the Kiowa, Companche and Apache tribes, the document being dated January 23, 1900.

MR. BARNEY: No objection

COMMISSIONER O'MARR: It may be received.

(The said exhibit, Plaintiffs' Exhibit No. 42, admitted in evidence, is included in the "Book of Exhibits" comprising a part of this transcript, at page number 46 thereof.)

MR. THOMPSON: I offer in evidence, as Plaintiffs' Exhibit No. 43, Senate 255, 56th Congress, 1st Session, being the Fort Hall bill as it appears in the House of Representatives, dated January 30, 1900.

MR. BARNEY: No objection.

COMMISSIONER O'MARR: It may be received.

(The said Exhibit, Plaintiffs' Exhibit No. 43, admitted in evidence, is included in the "Book of Exhibits" comprising a part of this transcript, at page number 47 thereof.)

MR. THOMPSON: I offer in evidence, as Plaintiffs' Exhibit No. 44, H. R. 8590, in the House of Representatives, 56th Congress, 1st Session, as that bill was reported from the House Indian Affairs Committee by Mr. Stephens on February 15, 1900.

MR. BARNEY: No objection.

COMMISSIONER O'MARR: It may be received.

(The said exhibit, Plaintiffs' Exhibit No. 44, admitted in evidence, is included in the "Book of Exhibits," comprising a part of this transcript, at page number 48 thereof.)

MR. THOMPSON: I offer in evidence, as Plaintiffs' Exhibit No. 45, the accompanying report, House Report No. 342, to the preceding exhibit, being dated February 15, 1900.

MR. BARNEY: No objection.

COMMISSIONER O'MARR: It may be received.

(The said exhibit, Plaintiffs' Exhibit No. 45, admitted in evidence, is included in the "Book of Exhibits," comprising a part of this transcript, at page number 49 thereof.)

MR. THOMPSON: I offer in evidence, as Plaintiffs' Exhibit No. 46, Senate Document No. 170, 56th Congress, 1st Session, being a document printed under date of February 14, 1900, presented by Mr. Harris, and concerning the ratification of Agreement with the Kiowa, Comanche, and Apache Indians, containing numerous resolutions presented to the

Congress, and, among other things, a detailed, section by section, analysis of the lands, the timbers and water contained thereon, and numerous affidavits submitted by citizens and other interested parties, concerning this legislation.

MR. BARNEY: The defendant desires to object to the various affidavits and reports, and requests the Commission to withhold its ruling and the objection will be made at the same time as the objection on Exhibit No. 39.

COMMISSIONER O'MARR: The ruling on the objection of the defendant will be reserved.

(The said exhibit, Plaintiffs' Exhibit No. 46, offered in evidence but to which objection was made and ruling reserved, is included in the "Book of Exhibits" comprising a part of this transcript, at page number 50 thereof.)

MR. THOMPSON: I next offer in evidence, as Plaintiffs' Exhibit No. 47, Senate Document No. 170, Part 2, of the 56th Congress, 1st session, being a document printed in the Senate of the United States under date of March 3, 1900, being presented by Mr. Harris, and being additional papers pertaining to the ratification of this agreement, one being a letter of Judge Townsend to Hon. John M. Thurston, United States senator; another a letter from Hon. Jno. H. Burford, Chief Justice of the Supreme Court of Oklahoma; another being a letter by Jno. L. McAtee, Associate Justice, Supreme Court of Oklahoma, and other papers, affidavits and documents pertaining to the legislation, history and the protests of Indians and other parties to the ratification of the Jerome Agreement.

MR. BARNEY: The defendant will desire to make the same objections and requests that the Commission reserve the ruling.

COMMISSIONER O'MARR: The ruling on the objection will be reserved.

(The said exhibit, Plaintiffs' Exhibit No. 47, offered in evidence, but to which objection was made and ruling reserved, is included in the "Book of Exhibits" comprising a part of this transcript, at page number 51 thereof.)

MR. THOMPSON: I desire to offer in evidence, as Plaintiffs' Exhibit No. 48, Senate Bill 255, 56th Congress, 1st Session, as that bill was reported in the House from the House Indian Affairs Committee, under date of February 22, 1900, this being the bill to ratify the Fort Hall agreement.

MR. BARNEY: No objection.

COMMISSIONER O'MARR: It may be admitted.

(The said exhibit, Plaintiffs' Exhibit No. 48, admitted in evidence as shown above, is included in "Book of Exhibits" comprising a part of this transcript, at page number 52 thereof.)

MR. THOMPSON: The preceding exhibit had with it an accompanying report in the House of Representatives, No. 419. The plaintiffs' attorneys have been unable to procure a copy of that report, but request permission at this time to procure a copy of it and insert it in the record at this place, with consent of Government counsel, as Plaintiffs' Exhibit 49, in order to preserve the continuity. I presume that there will be no objection to it?

MR. BARNEY: I can't tell until I see the type of report it is. Suppose that we have it understood that if I have any objection to it, I will include it with the written objection I file with the other documents.

MR. THOMPSON: That, of course, is agreeable.

COMMISSIONER O'MARR: If there are no objections filed, it will be admitted, as far as we are concerned.

(NOTE BY REPORTER: Said exhibit has not, at the time of transcribing this record, been handed to the reporter, but if and when same has been secured and furnished to the reporter it will be included in the "Book of Exhibits," at page number 53 thereof.)

MR. THOMPSON: I next offer in evidence, as Plaintiffs' Exhibit No. 50, H. R. 8590, 56th Congress, 1st Session, being an Act to Ratify and Confirm the Jerome Agreement, as it is printed in the Senate of the United States on March 6, 1900.

MR. BARNEY: No objection.

COMMISSIONER O'MARR: It may be received.

(The said exhibit, Plaintiffs' Exhibit No. 50, admitted in evidence, is included in the "Book of Exhibits," comprising a part of this transcript, at page number 54 thereof.)

MR. THOMPSON: I introduce, as Plaintiffs' Exhibit No. 51, Senate Document No. 26, 58th Congress, 2nd Session, being the Senate Report, and constituting a letter from the Secretary of the Interior, and transmitting to the Senate the results of an investigation into the affairs of the Kiowa Indian Agency, conducted by Francis E. Leupp, who was a Special Supervisor of Education, designated by the Secretary of the Interior to investigate the affairs of the Kiowa Indian Agency.

MR. BARNEY: No objection.

COMMISSIONER O'MARR: It will be admitted.

(The said exhibit, Plaintiffs' Exhibit No. 51, admitted in evidence as shown above, is included in the "Book of Exhibits" comprising a part of this transcript, at page number 55 thereof.)

MR. THOMPSON: I offer in evidence, as Plaintiffs' Exhibit No. 52, Senate Document No. 341, 57th Congress, 1st Session, being the report of W. A. Richards, Assistant

Commissioner of the General Land Office, respecting the opening of Kiowa, Comanche, and Apache and Wichita lands in Oklahoma; the document being dated May 5, 1902, and I may state, by way of further introduction, that this has to do with the opening of these lands to white settlement in 1901 when we had the lottery down here at Lawton and the names were drawn, the amount that was sold, the selling of town sites, and incidentally I may state that the document shows the total net receipt of $724,917.62 from the 960 acres that was sold to set up the town sites.

MR. BARNEY: No objection.

COMMISSIONER O'MARR: It may be received.

(The said exhibit, Plaintiffs' Exhibit No. 52, admitted in evidence, is included in the "Book of Exhibits," comprising a part of this transcript, at page number 56 thereof.)

MR. THOMPSON: In connection with Plaintiffs' Exhibit No. 6, Senate Document 77, it will be noted on page 2 of that exhibit, that at that date, namely: January 26, 1899, there appears to be a protest of the Indians which had been transmitted by Lt. Scott, which had been lost and was not available and was not printed as a part of this record. We have located the lost report and at this time I desire to offer in evidence, as Plaintiffs' Exhibit No. 53, a four page document, taken from the National Archives, being a copy of a protest, dated May 11, 1893, addressed by certain Kiowa, Comanche, and Kiowa Indians to the President of the United States, and a letter of transmittal to the Secretary of War by H. L. Scott, transmitting the protest, and ask that it be received in evidence as Plaintiffs' exhibit, as indicated.

 MR. BARNEY: No objection.

 COMMISSIONER O'MARR: It may be received.

(The said Exhibit, Plaintiffs' Exhibit No. 53, admitted in evidence, is included in the "Book of Exhibits" comprising a part of this transcript, at page number 57 thereof.)

 MR. THOMPSON: The plaintiffs offer in evidence, as Plaintiffs' Exhibit No. 54, pages numbered 1 through 97, inclusive, and including the certificate of the witnesses, interpreter, and agent on page 10, and the backing page, indicating the nature of the document. I may state, by way of support of the offer, that this is a photostatic copy of the Annuity Pay-Roll, which shows the per capita payment of $13.75 to every member of the Kiowa, Comanche, and Apache tribes, indicating their age and their sex, and running from a time starting on January 31, 1893, and concluding on February 10, 1893. I said that these pages were a photostatic copy of the records from the Indian Agent here, and a correction should be made in that statement. The local office did not contain pages 9 and 10, but those pages were procured from the records of the National Archives, and for purposes of convenience and uniformity they have been photographed and have been inserted in their proper place. Government counsel has been advised of the discrepancy. I will have an accompanying exhibit which will show the final wind-up of the Pay-Roll. It seems that a supplement was necessary in 1896 to pay some of the Indians who, though listed on this pay-roll, were not in attendance and were not paid until later. We will introduce that merely for the purpose of completing the record, and make the offer as Plaintiffs' Exhibit 54-A of an Annuity Pay-Roll, being two pages, together with an additional page containing the certificates of witnesses, interpreter and agent, and the backing sheet.

MR. BARNEY: I suppose we have no particular objection, Your Honors, but from the statement of counsel, it seems that the matter is hardly relevant. It purports to be the Annuity Pay-Roll, commencing with January 31, 1893, and running to June of the same year.

MR. THOMPSON: No, February 10th.

MR. BARNEY: I have no particular objection to it.

COMMISSIONER O'MARR: Gentlemen, I do not see the relevancy of it, but if there is no objection, it will be received.

MR. THOMPSON: Are you objecting?

MR. BARNEY: Yes, I guess I am.

MR. THOMPSON: Would you care to hear argument on it?

COMMISSIONER O'MARR: Very well, go ahead.

MR. THOMPSON: If Your Honors please, this is within three months of the date of this Agreement. This is the first census.

COMMISSIONER O'MARR: This isn't a census.

MR. THOMPSON: The first pay-roll, which indicates the age and sex of each of these Indians, and within three months of the time when the matter is at issue - (interrupted)

COMMISSIONER O'MARR: I appreciate the relevancy of it now. The objection will be overruled. It will be received.

(The said exhibits, Plaintiffs' Exhibits No. 54 and 54-A, admitted in evidence, are included in and comprise the "Supplement to Book of Exhibits" being a part of this transcript; Exhibit No. 54 being pages numbered 1 to 99 and Exhibit 54-A being pages numbered 100 to 103, of said Supplement to Book of Exhibits, the said exhibits being too bulky to include in the original "Book of Exhibits," it was necessary, for convenience in handling, to make a separate book of said exhibits.)

MR. THOMPSON: We expect to have about four or five more documents, which have not come to hand, of the documentary evidence.

COMMISSIONER O'MARR: We will take an adjournment until tomorrow morning at 9:30 o'clock.

(Thereupon an adjournment was had until the hour of 9:30 o'clock, a.m., of Thursday, May 12, 1949. And thereafter, at the hour of 9:30 o'clock, a.m., of said May 12, 1949, this hearing was resumed, with all officers and counsel present as at the time of adjournment, and further proceedings were had as follows, to-wit:)

PROCEEDINGS OF THURSDAY, MAY 12, 1949

(Thereupon EDGAR MONETATHCHI was called as an interpreter, and was duly sworn by the court to act as such interpreter.)

EKIYOVEY, called as a witness on the part of plaintiffs, being by the court, through said interpreter, duly sworn to testify truth, the whole truth and nothing but truth, testified as follows, testifying through said interpreter, to-wit:

(NOTE BY REPORTER: See previous explaination of reporter with respect to questions directed to the witness through the interpreter in the third person, such as, "Ask him,"etc. and answers by the witness interpreted in the third person, such as, "He said," etc.)

DIRECT EXAMINATION

QUESTIONS BY MR. THOMPSON:

Q   State your name.

A   Ekiyovey.

Q   What is your tribe?

A   Comanche.

Q   What is your age?

A   Around 72 or 73, approximately, since I do not know for sure.

Q   Do you know about the Jerome Commission coming to your lands to treat with you for the sale?

A   I remember them coming here. I did not see them at first but all I remember was a short time later when I saw them, on account of I did not know any white people.

Q   What was your age when you saw these white people?

A   I don't know exactly my age.

Q   Were you married at that time?

A   No, sir, I was not married.

Q   What was your occupation at that time?

A   I was Quanah Parker's hired man. I did most of his chores. I herded cattle all over the ranch.

Q   What is the first thing you remember of the Jerome Commission when you saw the Jerome Commission?

A   He said, "Quanah Parker told the people, 'We are selling the grass on the land, not the land itself; the grass on the land for cattlemen to graze their cattle on. If they made the transaction, it was only for the sale of the grass, the top soil he has reference to, and not underneath the ground.

Q   Did you attend any of the Council meetings between the Jerome Commission and the Indians?

A   He said he was standing outside among the crowd, because the arbor or shed they had made for the meeting was over-crowded and he had to stand on the outside.

Q   Where was this meeting?

A   He says, the site was where the present railway lies and the pavement.

Q   Was it in the vicinity of Fort Sill?

A   He says it was just below - just northeast of the present Indian Comanche mission.

Q   What did he hear of what was said at the council
meeting when he was in attendance?

A   He said that from where he was standing there among
the crowd, in the crowd, that he saw Tabananaca arise from
his seat and said, "I will make a statement and I want you"
pointing to a white lady, "to stand up and talk." When
Tabananaca and the white lady arose to talk, Quanah Parker,
who was standing up across from them said to the white lady,
"You being a woman, you have no business in this meeting.
You go back to your seat and sit down." and she lowered her
head and walked back to her seat.

Q   Ask him what the white woman's name was if he knows.

A   I don't know her name at this time.

Q   Are you now able to identify this interpreter?

A   He says that he cannot know her English name because not
being able to speak English, he says he cannot know her name.

Q   Do you recognize the name of Emsy Smith?

A   He says he heard that she was called that. He did not
know that was her name as he did not know the English language.

Q   What happened next at the council meeting that he heard?

A   When Quanah Parker ordered the white lady to go back
to her seat and sit down, Tabananaca got up and said to
Quanah Parker, "You are not going to do as you please with
this land. I will do as I please with this land and I
will sell it for $1.25 an acre."   And he said

that an Indian stood up by the name of Pohocsoot - (interrupted)

REPORTER: Can you spell that name?

INTERPRETER: At that time the Indians could not know how to spell their names. They had no written language, wherefore you spell it from the way it sounds. P-o-h-o-c-s-o-o-t. (continuing answer) Pohocsoot told Tabananca that Quanah Parker is asking for more money than you are asking; that is obvious.

Q What was Quanah Parker asking for?

A Quanah Parker was asking for $2.50.

Q Who interpreted Quanah Parker's statements to the white men of the Commission?

A I do not know because there were several talking.

Q Was Edward L. Clark, or Nock tooah, present at the meeting?

A I saw him.

Q Is Nock tooah the Indian name for Edward L. Clark?

A I did not know him as Edward L. Clark. I only knew him as Nock tooah.

Q Did you sign the Jerome Agreement?

A Quanah Parker addressed the assembly and said "You people who do not want $1.25 and want the $2.50 will please sign here."

Q Did you then sign it?

A He said that when Quanah Parker made the explanation, that for the people who were opposed to $1.25 and would sign

for the $2.50 to sign here, then was when he went over to
the place where Quanah Parker designated for the $2.50 and
held the pencil or pen, or top of the pen, and when he held
it there some one went and made a cross for him. When that
was done, he walked on out.

Q   Was there any other Indian in the three tribes named
Ekiyovey?

A   No, sir.

Q   You may question.

    MR. BARNEY: No questions.

    INTERPRETER: He wishes to make a statement. He said
that when he got through signing and walked on out and mingled
with the crowd, he turned around and a man arose from the
crowd, stood up and pointed toward the direction of the present site of Fort Sill and said, "You people see that flag in
the pasture? That is how much land I am going to get. That
is where my red mare is going to graze for pasture." His
name was Howeah. He says, "that is all I know."

        WITNESS EXCUSED

HOVARETHKA, called as a witness on the part of plaintiffs, and the interpreter Edgar Monetathchi called to act as interpreter for this witness, and the witness being, through said interpreter duly sworn to testify truth, the whole truth and nothing but truth, testified through said interpreter as follows:

(NOTE BY REPORTER: See previous explanation of reporter with respect to questions directed to the witness through the interpreter in the third person, such as, "Ask him," etc, and answers by the witness interpreted in the third person, such as, "He said," etc.)

DIRECT EXAMINATION
QUESTIONS BY MR. THOMPSON:

Q   State your name.

A   Hovarethka.

Q   What is your tribe?

A   Comanche.

Q   What is your age?

A   92.

Q   Do you remember the Jerome Commission - do you remember when the Jerome Commission came to the Indian reservation?

A   I remember.

Q   What was your age at that time?

A   About 36 years of age.

Q   Were you then married?

A   Yes.

Q   Did you then have children?

A   No children.

Q   What was your occupation then?

A   I was a soldier, working for the army.

Q   What was the name of your organization?

A   I was in the calvary.

Q   Who was your commanding officer?

A   Captain Scott.

Q   Did you attend any of the meetings of the Jerome Commission?

A   I was there for a short while.

Q   Where was the meeting that you attended held?

A   He said that they had a meeting in a hile house - a hide or storage house, and that he was there. That was when he first came.

131

Q   Was the Jerome Commission there at the same time?

A   Yes.

Q   What did you hear take place at that meeting?

A   I do not know very much, but what short time I was there, I remember four different instances.

Q   Tell us about those instances.

A   He said that the first thing he remembers was seeing a white man standing up and telling them, "Now, if you sell the land now, you will receive money for it."

Q   What else did you hear?

A   He said that the white man further stated that, "If you do not sell this land, it will be taken away from you for nothing."

Q   How much money did the white man say the Indians would receive for the land?

A   He said that he did not give the amount they would get, but talked in this manner: That a great big wagon load would be full of money.

Q   Was this white man one of the Commissioners?

A   He said, "I do not know that the white man came from Washington, but I was told, I heard, that he was the man that came from Washington."

Q   Who interpreted the white man's statements to the Comanches?

A   Nocktooah.

Q   Is that the man that is known in English as Edward L. Clark?

A   Yes. He said he was sometimes addressed as "Doctor" because he practiced medicine among the Indians.

Q   Was the statement that was being interpreted by Nocktooah being addressed to the group of Indians that were assembled for the meeting?

A   Yes.

Q   Did you sign the Jerome Agreement?

A   No, sir.

Q   Is there any one else in the Kiowa, Comanche and Apache tribes that has the name of Hovarethka?

A   I do not know of any.

MR. THOMPSON: No further questions.

MR. BARNEY: No questions.

COMMISSIONER O'MARR: That is all.

WITNESS EXCUSED

MUTUHME, called as a witness on the part of plaintiffs, and the interpreter Edgar Monetathchi, previously sworn, was called to interpret for the witness, and the witness being duly sworn to testify truth, the whole truth and nothing but truth, testified through said interpreter as follows:

(NOTE BY REPORTER: See previous explanation of reporter with respect to questions directed to the witness through the interpreter in the third person, such as "Ask him" etc., and answers by the witness interpreted in the third person, such as, "He said," etc.)

DIRECT EXAMINATION

QUESTIONS BY MR. THOMPSON:

Q   What is your name?

A   Mutuhme.

Q   What is your tribe?

A   Comanche.

Q   How old are you, if you know?

A   I do not know my exact age.

Q   Do you remember the Jerome Commission coming to this reservation?

A   Yes.

Q   Where did they come?

A   I first heard of them there at the Three Stores.

Q   Where is the Three Stores?

A   He says, from the Comanche Mission across the small creek there.

Q   Did you attend any of the meetings of the Jerome Commission with the Indians?

A   He said, "I only attended the last day of the meeting and I remember pretty well what went on. The other meetings they held at night were held by the principal chiefs and I do not know of that.

Q   Were these other meetings held before the one you attended?

A   Before. I heard that they held meetings at night before the time I attended the meeting.

Q   Tell us what you remember that took place in the meeting that you attended.

A   He says, "I will start from there. I will not tell it another way, other than the way what I saw and who I heard."

Q   Tell him that is all we want to hear.

A   He said that he was there at the meeting and "I heard there where they appraised the land. I was sitting there." He says, "I will tell you exactly what I saw and what I heard." He said that there was perfect stillness, as solemn as in a church, because they felt the presence of these important men there.

Q   Were these important men the Jerome Commissioners?

A   He says white men like him were there.

Q   Meaning me?

INTERPRETER: Yes.

Q   Is that all he heard?

A   He says, "I am listening closely, as I saw the picture. Tabananaca was standing up to my right. Quanah Parker was sitting to my left. Sitting beside him was Nocktooah." He said, "As I was sitting there, I was listening to them talk. If I had known the English language, I would have understood better what they were saying, but I can only state what I heard through my native tongue. Tabananaca was the chief. Tabananaca told them, 'We are going to sell our land,' and he was conducting the meeting." He said that the way he heard Tabananaca, he was speaking his tongue -"he was speaking my language and I understood him to say this, that we are going to sell our land for $1.25 an acre. He said, "I was curious to know, to hear what the white man would interpret the words that Tabananaca said in our language and I wish I could have understood what the white man was saying. That was the reason why I was there." He said, "I was sitting there among the crowd of Tabananaca followers. I did not know at the time that I was to be asked to sign the treaty or the agreement.

Q   Did not Quanah Parker say anything?

A   He said that when Tabananaca told the people that they were going to sell the land -- he gives a description of Tabananaca as being a real Indian, as being partially bald, and a handsome looking Indian man. Quanah Parker, he heard him say these words, he jumped up, held up his hands, and said, "Wait, that is not enough. The value of our lands is much greater." He said, "that white man" referring to Quanah Parker as a white man.

Q   Why did he refer to Quanah Parker as a white man?

A   Because Quanah Parker had a white man's ways, and because he was a smart man. Quanah Parker was a smart man was the reason why they called him a white man.

Q   What happened next?

A   When Quanah Parker voiced his opposition, Tabananaca got up and told him to sit down and said "White man, you are not going to do as you please with this land. It is my land. This is my people. I am going to do what I please with it," is what Tabananaca told Quanah Parker.

Q   Then what happened?

A   He said that Quanah Parker immediately sat down, when Tabananaca told him that, because Tabananaca was the chief. He said that because Quanah Parker didn't do right, because he was smart. He said that Tabananaca told the people the white men have agreed to my terms. "This is my land, I will do as I please with it. You are my people, my children. You will do as I say. We are going to touch this pencil, or pen, and make our cross marks there, and the white men were facing toward the sun. Tabananaca was standing to the white men's left.

Q   Did you hear an Indian named Howeah make a statement?
A   He said that without a mistake he heard the things that were spoken there.

Q   What did he hear said there?
A   When Tabananaca told his people, his followers, to sign, that they were going to sign with a pencil or pen, an Indian by the name of Howeah, standing to the back of Emsy Smith, the white lady that Quanah told to sit down, stood up and told Tabananaca, "You cannot persuade these people," pointing to me, "There is a young man we can refer to who is nice looking, intelligent fellow."

Q   Then what happened?
A   He says that when Howeah made that remark about Mutuhme, Tabananaca says, "How about it, son. Come here." and he says "I arose and also went to him."

Q   And then what happened?
A   When he got up and went over to where Tabananaca was, Howeah sat down and a question was asked him, "How old are you?"

Q   Who asked "How old are you?"
A   The white man that had the papers for them to sign asked the interpreter or some one to ask him how old he was. He does not know the person who asked the question.

Q   And what did you answer?
A   He said that the interpreter told him that they wanted to find out his age and he replied that he was around

eighteen years of age.

Q And what was the answer to that reply?

A "You are well qualified to sign."

Q And did you then sign?

A Yes, I signed. I held the pen or pencil in my hand and some one guided it to a cross mark.

Q No further questions. His number is 231 on Plaintiffs' Exhibit 5, "Moth tem my" and I would like to ask whether that is a variation of the spelling of this witness' name. Could you ask the witness that question?

INTERPRETER: Well, sir, I don't know whether he could distinguish, since the Comanche language is unwritten, but I will ask the question -- I don't know how to put it to him.

MR. THOMPSON: Then you can't ask him the question if you don't know how to put it to him.

Q Was there any other Indian in the three tribes at that time whose name was pronounced Mutuhme?

A I know of no one. I am the only one.

MR. THOMPSON: (To interpreter) Will you pronounce the name opposite 231 on Plaintiffs' Exhibit 5?

INTERPRETER: Mutuhme (pronouncing name)

MR. THOMPSON: Let the record show that the interpreter was asked to pronounce the name appearing opposite 231 on Plaintiffs' Exhibit 5, and the witness' name as put into the record at the beginning of his testimony and spelled M-u-t-u-h-m-e (spelling) and that the pronunciation was identically the same phonetically.

CROSS EXAMINATION

QUESTIONS BY MR. BARNEY:

Q   Did Mutuhme (witness) complete his statement of what happened when he went up to talk to Tabananaca after somebody asked him how old he was? Did anything happen after that?

A   He said that he did not state anything further because "I was only doing what they asked me. I was only answering their questions. They were the ones directing the meeting."

Q   After he told the interpreter that he was eighteen and they told him he was well qualified to sign, then what happened?

A   He said that "After I signed, I went back to my seat and Nocktooah got up and shouted. He said that Nocktooah got up and shouted, "It is a lot of money. Lots of bags full of money. Maybe it will fill one or two army wagon loads of money." That is what Nocktooah said. That is what he heard.

Q   Now, when Tabananaca said he wanted his people to sign, did they sign then?

A   Yes, we signed then, when he told us to. I am not going to tell what is over there. I am only going to tell what I know.

Q   Ask him how many people he saw sign, or touch the pen?

A   He says, "I do not know. There were a great many. They were taking turns signing. As I was sitting toward the back, I could not see them actually sign."

Q   But they were going up - (interrupted)

A   He says it cannot be determined how many signed.

Q   But he did see lots of people sign?

A   He said he saw them get up; he saw them bend over; he did not see them sign.

Q   That is all. Thank you very much.

WITNESS EXCUSED

MR. THOMPSON: I may state at the outset a situation that pertains to the next exhibits which I will introduce. On March 27, 1934, Congress passed an Act declaring that the Oklahoma Historical Society, located at Oklahoma City, should henceforth be the depository for old Indian records located, among other places, at the Kiowa Indian Agency at Anadarko. The documents which I intend to introduce at this time all are taken from the files of the Oklahoma Historical Society, and each one is under the seal and the signature of the Secretary to the Oklahoma Historical Society, attesting to their authenticity and the protecting custody that they have had since that organization took control.

141

I offer, as Plaintiffs' Exhibit No. 55, Instructions from T. J. Morgan, Commissioner of Indian Affairs, dated June 23, 1892, purportedly to the local agents and directing them how to prepare their annual report for the year ending August 30, 1892. Also contained in this exhibit is the report for the year ending August 30, 1892, which contains certain statistics with reference to the affairs of the tribe, including population figures.

MR. BARNEY: No objection.

COMMISSIONER O'MARR: It may be received.

(The Plaintiff's Exhibit No. 55, admitted in evidence, as shown above is included in "Book of Exhibits" at page number ___59___ thereof.)

MR. THOMPSON: I next offer in evidence, as Plaintiffs' Exhibit No. 56, a hand-written document, taken from the Oklahoma Historical Society, being headed, on Page 1, as follows: "Annual Report of the Kiowa Agency," bearing date September 1, 1892, and containing at page 7-3, a separate page, which page is dated September 13, 1892, and which gives a break-down of the population of the tribe from school schildren and adults, and as between males and females as of this date.

MR. BARNEY: No objection.

COMMISSIONER O'MARR: It may be received.

(The plaintiffs' Exhibit No. 56, admitted in evidence, is included in the "Book of Exhibits" comprising a part of this transcript, at page number 60 thereof.)

MR. THOMPSON: I next offer in evidence, as Plaintiffs' Exhibit No. 57, the extracts from the printed report of the Agent for August 30, 1892, as it appears in the report of the Secretary of the Interior, 1892, also under the seal of the Oklahoma Historical Society.

MR. BARNEY: No objection.

COMMISSIONER O'MARR: It may be received.

(The said exhibit, Plaintiffs' Exhibit No. 57, admitted in evidence, is included in the "Book of Exhibits" comprising a part of this transcript, at page number 61 thereof.)

MR. THOMPSON: I offer in evidence, as Plaintiffs' Exhibit No. 58, a typewritten copy of a protest signed by a certain number of Indians, being 14 pages in length, and the last page of the exhibit being under the signature of Frank D. Baldwin, Acting Indian Agent, all being under the certificate of the Oklahoma Historical Society.

MR. BARNEY: No objection.

COMMISSIONER O'MARR: It may be received.

(The Plaintiffs' Exhibit No. 58, admitted in evidence as shown above, is included in "Book of Exhibits," at page number __62__ thereof.)

MR. THOMPSON: I offer, as Plaintiffs' Exhibit No. 59, a certified copy of a protest dated May 8, 1899, signed by certain Indians, being addressed to the Honorable W. A. Jones, Commissioner of Indian Affairs, Washington, D.C., protesting against the Jerome Agreement.

MR. BARNEY: No objection.

COMMISSIONER O'MARR: Nm It may be received.

(The Plaintiffs' Exhibit No. 59, admitted in evidence as shown above, is included in "Book of Exhibits," at page number __63__ thereof.)

MR. BARNEY: With reference to Plaintiffs' Exhibit

No. 58, the defendant makes no objection to the document as such, but calls attention to the fact that it is not dated, and although it was described for purposes of identification by counsel for the plaintiffs, of March 1, 1894, it is apparent on the face of the document that it couldn't have been dated March 1, 1894, because it refers in the body of the document to a Senate document which "Was referred to the Committee on Indian Affairs March 1, 1894." I will further state to the Commission that I have seen this document in the State Historical Society, and it doesn't bear any date, and I attempted to find out from the lady in charge, Mrs. Looney, if she had any idea of when this document - the date of it, and she was also unable to give me any information concerning it.

COMMISSIONER O'MARR: As long as it is subsequent to the signing of the treaty of 1892, it would be competent.

MR. BARNEY: Oh, yes. I am not making any objection to the competency of it, because it is obviously a government document.

COMMISSIONER O'MARR: The date wouldn't be very important, would it?

MR. BARNEY: I would think so. If it took place a long time after the happening of the transaction, it would be of less value, I think.

COMMISSIONER O'MARR: I think we have protests as late as 1899.

MR. BARNEY: I am merely calling the attention of the Commission to the fact that it is not dated and I have not, personally, been able to find out the date of it.

MR. THOMPSON: I might suggest that we have a short recess. I have a document which I must locate and we have a witness whom we expect most any moment.

COMMISSIONER O'MARR: Well, let us know, Mr. Thompson, when you are ready.

MR. THOMPSON: Yes, sir.

(Thereupon a recess was taken, the hour being 11:00 a.m., of May 12, 1949. And thereafter, at the hour of 11:50 o'clock, a.m., court reconvened and Commissioner O'Marr announced that a recess would be taken until the hour of 1:15 o'clock, p.m., of said day. And thereafter, at the hour of 1:25 o'clock, p.m., of said day court again reconvened with all officers and counsel present as before, and further proceedings were had as follows, to-wit:)

(Thereupon Edgar Monetathchi, an interpreter heretofore sworn to act as interpreter, was called to act as interpreter.)

MEAHKER, called as a witness by the plaintiffs, being, through said interpreter, first duly sworn to testify truth, the whole truth, and nothing but truth, testified as follows; testifying through said interpreter Edgar Monetathchi.:

(NOTE BY REPORTER: See previous explanation of reporter with respect to questions directed to the witness through the interpreter in the third person, such as, "Ask him," etc., and answers by the witness interpreted in the third person, such as "He said," etc.)

DIRECT EXAMINATION

QUESTIONS BY MR. THOMPSON:

Q State your name.

A Meahker.

Q What is your tribe?

A He says, "I am a Comanche."

Q How old are you?

A I do not know my exact age.

Q Did you learn that the Commission, called the Jerome Commission, came to this reservation to treat for the sale of your lands?

A I did not hear.

Q Did you ever learn that this Commission had come to the reservation?

A About five or six days later.

Q What was he doing when the Jerome Commission came to the reservation? What was his occupation?

A He said, "At the time I was farming and raising corn and just regular farm work."

Q Where were you farming and raising corn?

A He said that it was over there around Little Washita Creek

Q Did you attend any of the meetings of the Jerome Comsion?

A   No.

Q   Did you sign the Jerome Agreement?

A   No.

Q   Is there any other Indian in the three tribes who has the same name that you have, "Meahker?"

A   I know of no one having my name.

Q   No further questions.

    MR. BARNEY: No questions.

WITNESS EXCUSED

    MR. THOMPSON: May it please the Court, at this time I would like to announce that this concludes the testimony which we wish to present on the case at Lawton. This is not the formal closing of our case, but is all the testimony we now have available at this place.

    COMMISSIONER O'MARR: Very well then, we will adjourn until further notice.

    (Thereupon the hearing of this Case stood adjourned, purusant to the announcement of Commissioner O'Marr.)

BEFORE THE INDIAN CLAIMS COMMISSION

THE KIOWA, COMANCHE AND APACHE　）
TRIBES OF INDIANS,　　　　　　　　　　）
　　　　　　　　　Petitioners,　　　　）
　　　　　　　　　　　　　　　　　　　）
　　Vs.　　　　　　　　　　　　　　　）　　Docket No. 32
　　　　　　　　　　　　　　　　　　　）
THE UNITED STATES OF AMERICA,　　　　）
　　　　　　　　　　　　　　　　　　　）
　　　　　　　　　Defendant.　　　　　）

CERTIFICATE OF COURT REPORTER

I, Archie McInnes, hereby CERTIFY that on the 9th, 10th, 11th and 12th days of May, 1949, after the Clerk of the aforesaid Commission administered the oath to me, I reported in shorthand all of the proceedings had and done at Lawton, Oklahoma in the above entitled matter, and later transcribed said notes into typewriting; that the within and foregoing is a full, true, correct and complete transcript of my shorthand notes of said proceedings.

Dated at Oklahoma City, Oklahoma, this ~~30~~th day of September, 1949.

　　　　　　　　　　　　　　　　Archie McInnes, Court Reporter
　　　　　　　　　　　　　　　　307 County Courthouse,
　　　　　　　　　　　　　　　　Oklahoma City 2, Oklahoma

Subscribed and sworn to before me, this the 28th day of September, 1949.

　　　　　　　　　　　　　　　　Notary Public in and for
　　　　　　　　　　　　　　　　the State of Oklahoma

My Commission Expires:
Jan 4- 1953

BEFORE THE
INDIAN CLAIMS COMMISSION
OF THE UNITED STATES

- - - - - - - - - - - - - - - - *

THE KIOWA, COMANCHE AND APACHE :
TRIBES OF INDIANS, :
 :
          Petitioners :
 :
vs. : No. 32
 :
THE UNITED STATES OF AMERICA, :
 :
          Defendant. :
 :
- - - - - - - - - - - - - - - - *

Washington, D. C.,
Tuesday, October 4, 1949,
10:00 o'clock, a.m.

The parties met, pursuant to the notice of the Commission, at the time above stated, in the hearing room of the Indian Claims Commission:

BEFORE:

    Hon. Edgar E. Witt, Chief Commissioner;
    Hon. William M. Holt, Associate Commissioner; and
    Hon. Louis J. O'Marr, Associate Commissioner.

APPEARANCES:

    William C. Lewis, Esq., and
    J. Roy Thompson, Esq., Counsel for Petitioners;

    Julius Martin II, Esq., Counsel for Defendant.

    Kenneth K. Johnston, reporter, was duly sworn to well and truly take down and transcribe the questions put to and the replies given by the witness, and to do all other things required by the members of the Commission.

COMMISSIONER WITT: I guess we are ready to proceed, gentlemen.

MR. THOMPSON: May it please the Court, on behalf of the Petitioners in this case we have some additional documentary evidence which we would like to offer this morning. It is supplementary of the evidence which has been previously introduced, and will, we believe, enable the Commissioners to get the entire story.

At this time Petitioners offer in evidence as Petitioners' Exhibit No. 60, a document composed of pages 5-1 through 5-6, together with a backing sheet, which paper is taken from the National Archives, and is a letter from the Acting Secretary of the Interior to the President, dated May 23, 1887, recommending the allotment of the lands in question to the Indians.

COMMISSIONER WITT: Are you submitting this?

MR. THOMPSON: Yes, sir.

COMMISSIONER WITT: Will you submit it to counsel for the Government?

MR. THOMPSON: It has been submitted to him.

MR. MARTIN: There is no objection.

COMMISSIONER:WITT: Admitted.

(Document marked Pages 5-1 through 5-6 and backing sheet, being letter from Acting Secy. of Interior to Commissioner of Indian Affairs, dated June 10, 1887 with enclosure being letter from

Secretary of Interior to the President, dated May 23, 1887, were marked "Petitioners' Exhibit No. 60," and made a part of this record.)

MR. THOMPSON: I may state further that the approval is dated June 4, 1887, and is in the hand signature of Grover Cleveland.

I next offer in evidence as Petitioners' Exhibit No. 61, a series of papers which are pertinent extracts from the instructions which were given to the Cherokee Commission, prepared by the Commissioner of Indian Affairs, prior to their visit to Oklahoma to negotiate for these lands.

COMMISSIONER WITT: What Commission did you say?

MR. THOMPSON: The Cherokee Commission, which is colloquially called the Jerome Commission. They are the same.

I have extracted from the records of the National Archives those portions which seem pertinent to the Kiowa, Comanche and Apache lands. As a part of the offer I would call the attention of the Commission to the fact that commencing on numbered page 78 there is a typewritten portion which follows clear through to the conclusion, which is called "Instructions and Suggestions." That will be pertinent to the next offer that I desire to make.

MR. MARTIN: What is the date?

COMMISSIONER WITT: Any objection?

MR. MARTIN: No objection, but I would like to have the

date.

MR. THOMPSON: The date of the transmission from the Commissioner of Indian Affairs to the Secretary of the Interior is May 9, 1887.

>(Letter dated May 9, 1887 from Commissioner of Indian Affairs to Secy. of the Interior, together with extracts from the instructions given to the Cherokee Commission, were marked "Petitioners' Exhibit No. 61," and made a part of this record.)

MR. THOMPSON: I offer in evidence as Petitioners' Exhibit No. 62 a letter from John W. Noble, the Secretary of the Interior, to Horace Speed, the Secretary, Cherokee Commission, dated July 6, 1889, by which the Secretary of the Interior transmitted to the Cherokee Commission the instructions which have been referred to in the previous exhibit.

COMMISSIONER WITT: Admitted.

>(Letter dated 7-6-89 from Secy. of Interior Noble, to Horace Speed, Secy., Cherokee Commission, was marked "Petitioners' Exhibit No. 62," and made a part of this record.)

MR. THOMPSON: Now, may it please the Court, there came a time when there was a call by the Senate for the production of the instructions to this Commission, and in order to complete the chain of history I desire at this time to read from Senate Report No. 552, 52nd Congress, First Session, which was ordered to be printed April 13, 1892, pages 8 and 9.

(Reading:)

"On the 19th of December, 1889, the Senate adopted the following resolution:

"'Resolved, That the Secretary of the Interior be directed to send to the Senate the compilation recently made in the Indian Bureau concerning the legal status of the Indians and lands located in the Indian Territory, and that he also, if not incompatible with the public interest, send to the Senate instructions issued to the Commission recently appointed pursuant to act of Congress to negotiate for the cession to the Government of lands west of the ninety-sixth degree in the Indian Territory.'

"The Secretary, however, not only declined to send the 'instructions,' but also declined to send the 'compilation.' His answer to the resolution of the Senate is printed in Senate Ex. Doc. No. 21, first session, Fifty-first Congress, as follows:

"'Department of the Interior,
Washington, December 21, 1889.

"'Sir: I have the honor to acknowledge the receipt of the following resolution of the Senate, dated 19th instant:

"'Resolved, That the Secretary of the Interior be directed to send to the Senate the compilation recently made in the Indian Bureau concerning the legal status of the Indians and lands located in the Indian Territory, and that he also, if not incompatible with the public interest, send to the Senate instructions issued to the commission recently appointed pursuant to act of Congress to negotiate for the cession to the Government of lands west of the ninety-sixth degree in the Indian Terrirory.'

"'In response thereto I have the honor to state that no compilation has been made by the Indian Bureau concerning the legal status of the Indians and lands located in the Indian Territory other than that embodied in the instructions to the Cherokee Commission.

"'In view of the pending negotiations with these Indians, I deem it incompatible with the public interest that these instructions at this time be made public.

"'With the final report of the commission a copy of the instructions herewith requested will be furnished.

"'I have the honor to be, very respectfully,

"'John W. Noble, Secretary.'

"The President of the Senate."

COMMISSIONER WITT: Is that to be an exhibit?

MR. THOMPSON: I did not propose to introduce the volume in evidence, except that portion of it which pertains to the history of the instructions to the Cherokee Commission. However, I would be pleased to incorporate it in the record, if you desire to make it a Commission exhibit.

COMMISSIONER WITT: Whatever procedure you care to follow in the matter is satisfactory.

Any objection?

MR. MARTIN: No objection.

COMMISSIONER O'MARR: Those are the instructions referred to, which have been offered in evidence in the preceding exhibit; is that true?

MR. THOMPSON: Yes, in part. I will complete the chain with my next offer, and I will make an explanation so that it will be abundantly clear.

The Senate, in response to the proceedings which I have just read, passed a resolution demanding that the Secretary of the Interior produce the compilation, and the Secretary of the Interior did, in response to that resolution, produce the compilation, and it is set out in Senate Executive Doc. No. 78, 51st Congress, 1st Session, with an accompanying map.

But the Secretary of the Interior then did not transmit to the Senate what we call the secret instructions, which we have procured from the National Archives, and which form a part of a preceding exhibit. In other words, we get the entire picture by the admission of Senate Executive Doc. No. 78, with the accompanying map, plus the secret instructions which are not contained in this public document.

I offer this in evidence as Petitioners' Exhibit No. 63, with the accompanying map.

MR. MARTIN: Did you not put that other document in evidence, Mr. Thompson?

MR. THOMPSON: I did not put that in evidence but I read the portion which is pertinent.

MR. MARTIN: I beg your pardon.

COMMISSIONER WITT: Any objection?

MR. MARTIN: No objection.

COMMISSIONER WITT: It is admitted.

>(Letter from Secy. of Interior transmitting in response to Senate Resolution of March 10, 1890 Compilation concerning legal status of Indians in Indian Territory, together with attached map, were marked "Petitioners' Exhibit No. 63," and made a part of this record.)

MR. THOMPSON: I offer in evidence as Petitioners' Exhibit No. 64 the final report of the Cherokee or Jerome Commission, dated August 21, 1893, together with an accompanying schedule which summarizes the work of the Commission.

COMMISSIONER WITT: Any objection?

MR. MARTIN: No objection, if the Court please.

COMMISSIONER WITT: Admitted.

>(Report of Cherokee Commission dated August 21, 1893, together with accompanying schedule were marked "Petitioners' Exhibit No. 64," and made a part of this record.)

COMMISSIONER WITT: Just to expedite things, these matters might be considered as admitted, unless counsel for the Defendant makes some objection. Is that agreeable?

MR. MARTIN: Yes, sir, that will be satisfactory.

MR. THOMPSON: I offer as Petitioners' Exhibit No. 65

a letter from Charles C. Painter, Agent for the Indian Rights
Association, dated November 3, 1893, to Hon. D. M. Browning,
Commissioner of Indian Affairs. This letter makes reference
to enclosures, which enclosures have already been admitted
into evidence.

>(Letter from Chas. C. Painter, Agent
>Indian Rights Assoc., to D. M. Brown-
>ing, Commissioner of Indian Affairs,
>dated Nov. 3, 1893, was marked
>"Petitioners' Exhibit No. 65," and
>made a part of this record.)

MR. THOMPSON: I offer as Petitioners' Exhibit No. 66 a
copy of a letter from the National Archives by Frank D.
Baldwin, Captain, United States Army, who was acting agent
of the Kiowa Agency, the letter being dated March 29, 1897,
to the Committee on Indian Affairs through the offices of the
Hon. Commissioner of Indian Affairs and Secretary of the
Interior, having to do with the cession of these lands.

>(Letter dated March 29, 1897 from
>Capt. Frank D. Baldwin to Committee on
>Indian Affairs, House of Representa-
>tives, was marked "Petitioners' Exhibit
>No. 66," and made a part of this record.)

MR. THOMPSON: I next offer in evidence as Petitioners'
Exhibit No. 67 transcript of a conference between the Commiss-
ioner of Indian Affairs and the representatives of the Kiowa,
Comanche and Apache Indians of Oklahoma, in the office of
Indian Affairs, Washington, D. C., April 29, 1897.

>(Transcript of Conference between
>Commissioner of Indian Affairs and
>representatives of Kiowa, Comanche and
>Apache Indians of Oklahoma, dated

April 29, 1897, was marked "Petitioners' Exhibit No. 67," and made a part of this record.)

MR. THOMPSON: At this time I would like to read into the record an extract from the report of Frank D. Baldwin, Captain, Fifth Infantry, United States Army, Acting United States Indian Agent, being the Annual Report of Captain Baldwin to the Commissioner of Indian Affairs, dated August 28, 1897, which appears in the Annual Report of the Commissioner of Indian Affairs, 1897, commencing on page 231.

The extract which I shall read appears on page 233.

Captain Baldwin says:

"The question of opening these reservations to settlement by whites is one that causes constant uneasiness and an unsettled state of affairs. Having before them the deplorable condition of the Cheyenne and Arapaho Indians, as well as many other tribes whose lands have been taken from them under the form of a treaty and opened to settlement by whites, this is what they judge from and base their own possible conditions when their reservations are absorbed into the public domain. They are not unwilling to part with their surplus lands to their own people, that is, to Indians of other tribes, but they naturally, and for just reasons, dread the coming of that class of white people who are ever ready in their greed to pounce down upon them.

"As an example of their earnestness in this matter they

have consented to the adding of upward of 50,000 acres of land to the Fort Sill Military Reservation for use and occupancy of the Geronimo Apache prisoners, and have further expressed their unwillingness to sell to the Absentee Wyandottes sufficient lands so that each, to the number of 206 people, shall have 160 acres. This is all fully provided for by treaty, the terms of which they are willing and ready to comply with, and now they ask that the Government recognize its obligations under the same treaty and not confirm a treaty (the Jerome treaty) which was made and completed by coercion and fraud."

As the Commission will remember, the Act of Congress confirming and ratifying the so-called Jerome Agreement, and changes was approved by the President on June 6, 1900. I desire at this time to offer as Petitioners' Exhibit No. 68 a letter from the Secretary of the Interior to the President, dated May 15, 1900, with reference to this legislation.

(Letter dated May 15, 1900 from Secy. of Interior to the President in re ratification of Jerome Agreement, was marked "Petitioners' Exhibit No. 68," and made a part of this record.)

MR. THOMPSON: May it please the Court, at this time that concludes the evidence that the Petitioner has available. There are one and possibly two sources of original material that we have not yet fully exhausted. As the Commission can appreciate, the volume of documentary evidence in this case is enormous. We would like to close our case-in-chief at this time, however with the reservation that if, within a reasonable time which we can all agree on, we obtain documents from these sources, that we may be allowed to then hold another hearing for the consideration of same.

COMMISSIONER WITT: Any objection?

MR. MARTIN: No, sir, there is no objection on the part of Defendant. However, the Defendant would like to state that we have some testimony which we wish to offer this morning, and we would like, at the time Mr. Thompson for Petitioners brings in other evidence, to produce some things which we may wish to offer by way of rebuttal.

If the Commission please, one of the chief reasons for this is that we have just received a copy of the evidence taken in Lawton, Oklahoma, last May 9th, and of course I have not had an opportunity to read that, and I think we ought to have a reasonable opportunity to rebut some of that testimony that is in there.

COMMISSIONER WITT: I presume that is all right with counsel.

MR. THOMPSON: It is completely satisfactory.

COMMISSIONER WITT: The record will so show. Off the record, Mr. Reporter, please.

(Here followed discussion off the record.)

COMMISSIONER WITT: All right, Mr. Martin.

MR. MARTIN: If the Commission pleases, the Defendant

desires to offer at this time as Defendant's Exhibit No. 2
a certified copy of an affidavit filed in opposition to the
temporary injunction sought in the case of Lone Wolf against
Hitchcock, extracted by Ethan A. Hitchcock, then Secretary of
the Interior, on June 12, 1901, found in the original files of
the Supreme Court of the District of Columbia.

COMMISSIONER WITT: Any objection?

MR. THOMPSON: No objection.

COMMISSIONER WITT: These matters will be considered
admitted in evidence as offered, unless there is objection
made by Petitioners' counsel.

>(Certified copy of affidavit filed in
>Lone Wolf vs. Hitchcock case, dated
>June 12, 1901, was marked "Defendant's
>Exhibit No. 2," and made a part of
>this record.)

MR. MARTIN: The Defendant offers as its Exhibit No. 3
an excerpt from the Case of Choctaw and Chickasaw Nations
vs. the United States, 88 Court of Claims, 271, at page 281,
Finding No. 10.

>(Except from Case of Choctaw & Chickasaw
>Nations vs. U.S., 88 Court of Claims,
>271, p. 281, Finding No. 10, was marked
>"Defendant's Exhibit No. 3" and made a
>part of this record.)

MR. MARTIN: Defendant offers as its Exhibit No. 4,
31 Stat. 672, pages 676 to 678, on the Act of June 6, 1900,
being the Act ratifying the Jerome Agreement, a copy of that
to be supplied for the convenience of the Commission.

(Copy of pages 676-678 of 31 Stat. 672, was marked "Defendant's Exhibit No. 4," and will be furnished for the record.)

MR. MARTIN: Defendant offers as its Exhibit No. 5, 31 Stat. 727, being the Act of January 4, 1901, an Act authorizing the extension of time for allotments, a copy of which is to be supplied for the convenience of the Commission.

(Copy of 31 Stat. 727, Act of Jan. 4, 1901, authorizing extension of time for allotments, was marked "Defendant's Exhibit No. 5," and will be furnished for the record.)

MR. MARTIN: Defendant wishes to refer to the case of Lone Wolf against Hitchcock, No. 187 U.S. 553.

COMMISSIONER WITT: When you say you refer to the Lone Wolf case, what do you mean? Do you mean the opinion in the case?

MR. MARTIN: I call it to the attention of the Court.

COMMISSIONER WITT: The opinion in the case?

MR. MARTIN: Yes, sir.

That concludes what Defendant has to offer at this particular time.

COMMISSIONER WITT: Does that mean that concludes the testimony until a later date?

MR. MARTIN: Until the hearing on November 21st, yes, sir.

COMMISSIONER WITT: Court is adjourned.

(Whereupon, at 10:30 o'clock, adjournment was taken subject to the call of the Commission.)

-o-0-o-

CERTIFICATE OF REPORTER

I, Kenneth K. Johnston, reporter, hereby certify that at the time and place aforesaid, after being duly sworn by the Commissioner, I did well and truly take down and transcribe the proceedings as herein recorded; and that the foregoing record is a correct transcript of the proceedings so had therein.

In witness whereof, I have hereunto set my hand and seal this the 4th day of October, 1949.

Reporter - 727 19th St. NW,
Washington, D. C.

-- -- --

BEFORE THE
INDIAN CLAIMS COMMISSION
OF THE UNITED STATES

THE KIOWA, COMANCHE AND APACHE
TRIBES OF INDIANS,

          Petitioners

   vs.   NO. 32

THE UNITED STATES OF AMERICA,

          Defendant.

                            Washington, D. C.,
                            Monday, November 21, 1949,
                            10:00 o'clock, a.m.

The parties met, pursuant to the notice of the Commission, at the time above stated, in the hearing room of the Indian Claims Commission:

BEFORE:

    Hon. Edgar E. Witt, Chief Commissioner;
    Hon. William M. Holt, Associate Commissioner; and
    Hon. Louis J. O'Marr, Associate Commissioner.

APPEARANCES:

    J. Roy Thompson, Esq., Counsel for Petitioners;

    Ralph A. Barney, Esq., Counsel for Defendant; and
    Julius Martin II, Esq., Counsel for Defendant.

David L. Harrison, a reporter, was duly sworn to well and truly take down and transcribe the questions put to and the replies given by the witness, and to do all other things required by the members of the Commission.

COMMISSIONER WITT: Are we ready to proceed in No. 32?

MR. THOMPSON: If it please the Commission, I believe the state of the record was that the Defendant would proceed this morning with any evidence that they might have to offer and we would be allowed an opportunity to produce any evidence that we had, at the same time.

The petitioner states at the present time on the record that they have no further evidence to offer upon the case upon its merits.

MR. MARTIN: The Defendant has nothing further to offer in the case on its merits.

COMMISSIONER WITT: Did Plaintiff say they had nothing further to offer?

MR. THOMPSON: Yes, sir.

(Here followed discussion off the record.)

MR. THOMPSON: May it please the Commission, this question has been raised by the Defendant and the Petitioner is perfectly willing at this time to make the following statement on the record:

At the hearing in Oklahoma, Dr. Wardell testified there. His testimony comprised two main parts:

The first was with reference to the historical background of the relations with the Indians and the United States, relations to the Kowa, Comanche and Apache Indians.

On page 92 of the transcript, as filed herein, Dr. Wardell testified with respect to land values around 1900.

At the conclusion of that testimony and after the cross examination on page 134 of the transcript, there was a motion made to strike the evidence relative to land values, which motion was not passed upon, but was held in abeyance at the request of the Petitioner's counsel.

The Petitioner here desires to state that this testimony with reference to land values, specifically commencing on page 92, is no part of the Petitioner's case on the merits and the Petitioner is not now requesting a rule upon the land valuation. If and when we get to the point of valuation, the testimony here will be sought to be incorporated in the record, but for the purposes of the hearing on the merits, that part of the testimony of Dr. Wardell is not to be considered.

MR. BARNEY: Under those circumstances, the Government does not insist at this time on a ruling on its motion to strike, which was reserved, but we reserve the right to renew the motion if and when the testimony is sought to be used hereafter.

COMMISSIONER WITT: Is there anything further?

MR. THOMPSON: With reference to the proposed findings, the record in this case is voluminous and Petitioner would request that he be granted 60 days within which to make his proposed findings.

    COMMISSIONER WITT: From this date?

    MR. THOMPSON: Yes, from this date.

    COMMISSIONER O'MARR: You have that under the rules?

    MR. BARNEY: 45; is it not?

    COMMISSIONER O'MARR: 40.

Is there any objection?

    MR. BARNEY: No objection. The Government would like to have an equal length of time, 20 days additional, or 60 days.

    MR. THOMPSON: No objection.

I have nothing further.

    MR. BARNEY: There is nothing further.

    COMMISSIONER WITT: The hearing is adjourned.

    (Whereupon, at 10:15 o'clock, the hearing was closed.)

-o-0-o-

CERTIFICATE OF REPORTER

I, David L. Harrison, Reporter, hereby certify that at the time and place aforesaid, after being duly sworn by the Commissioner, I did well and truly take down and transcribe the proceedings as herein recorded; and that the foregoing record is a correct transcript of the proceedings so had therein.

In witness whereof, I have hereunto set my hand and seal, this the 28th day of November, 1949.

Reporter, 727 19th St. N. W.,
Washington, D. C.

COMMISSION FINDINGS

See also Findings in *Caddoan Indians IV* and in *Apache Indians XII* (particularly 12 ICC 439 and 12 ICC 470) in the Garland American Indian Ethnohistory Series.

BEFORE THE INDIAN CLAIMS COMMISSION

THE KIOWA, COMANCHE, AND)
APACHE TRIBES OF INDIANS,)
)
     Petitioners,   )
)
        v.   )   Docket No. 32
)
THE UNITED STATES OF AMERICA,)
)
     Defendant.   )

APR 9 1951

FINDINGS OF FACT

The Commission makes the following findings of fact in the above-entitled cause:

1. The petitioners herein, the Kiowa, Comanche, and Apache Tribes of Indians, acquired the lands involved in this claim in the following manner:

On the 21st day of October, 1867, 15 Stat. 581, the Kiowa and Comanche Tribes of Indians entered into a treaty with the United States by which the United States ceded to said tribes, the Kiowa and Comanche, the following described territory located in what is now the State of Oklahoma, to-wit:

"commencing at a point where the Washita River crosses the 98th meridian, west from Greenwich; thence up the Washita River, in the middle of the main channel thereof, to a point thirty miles, by river, west of Fort Cobb, as now established; thence, due west to the north fork of Red River, provided said line strikes said river east of the one hundredth meridian of west longitude; if not, then only to said meridian-line, and thence south, on said meridian-line, to the said north fork of Red River; thence down said north fork, in the middle of the main channel thereof, from the point where it may be first intersected by the lines above described, to the main Red River;

171

thence down said river, in the middle of the main channel thereof to its intersection with the ninety-eighth meridian of longitude west from Greenwich; thence north, on said meridian-line, to the place of beginning, * * *."

On the same day (15 Stat. 589) the United States and the Kiowa, Comanche, and Apache Tribes of Indians concluded a treaty by the terms of which the Apache Tribe united with the other two tribes and thereby acquired an interest in the above-described lands; so, thereafter the three tribes became the owners of said lands.

The above-mentioned treaties were duly ratified by the Senate of the United States, and said Indians occupied the territory ceded to them following the ratification of said treaties.

2. Pursuant to section 14 of the Act of March 2, 1889, 25 Stat. 980, the President of the United States appointed a Commission, comprised of David H. Jerome, Chairman, Warren G. Sayre and Alfred M. Wilson, to negotiate an agreement with petitioners for the cession of their lands described in Finding 1 hereof, and pursuant to said Act said Commissioners negotiated an agreement with said three tribes of Indians on the 6th day of October, 1892, which agreement became historically known as the Jerome Agreement, and is in words and figures as follows:

    Articles of Agreement made and entered into at Fort Sill, in the Indian Territory, on the
by and between David H. Jerome, Alfred M. Wilson and Warren G. Sayre, Commissioners on the part of the United States, and the Commanche, Kiowa and Apache Tribes of Indians, in the Indian Territory.

ARTICLE I

Subject to the allotment of land in severalty to the individual members of the Commanche, Kiowa and Apache Tribes of Indians in the Indian Territory, as hereinafter provided for, and subject to the conditions hereinafter imposed, and for the considerations hereinafter mentioned, the said Commanche, Kiowa and Apache Indians hereby cede, convey, transfer, relinquish and surrender, forever and absolutely, without any reservation whatever, express or implied, all their claim title and interest, of every kind and character, in and to the lands embraced in the following described tract of country in the Indian Territory; to wit, Commencing at a point where the Washita River crosses the ninety-eighth meridian west from Greenwich; thence up the Washita River, in the middle of the main channel thereof, to a point thirty miles, by river, west of Fort Cobb, as now established; thence due west to the north fork of Red River, provided said line strikes said river east of the one-hundredth meridian of west longitude; if not, then only to said meridian line, and thence due south, on said meridian line, to the said north fork of Red River; thence down said north fork, in the middle of the main channel thereof, from the point where it may be first intersected by the lines above described, to the main Red River; thence down said Red River, in the middle of the main channel thereof, to its intersection with the ninety-eighth meridian of longitude west from Greenwich; thence north, on said meridian line, to the place of beginning.

ARTICLE II.

Out of the lands ceded, conveyed, transferred, relinquished and surrendered by Article I. hereof, and in part consideration for the cession thereof, it is agreed by the United States that each member of said Commanche, Kiowa and Apache Tribes of Indians over the age of eighteen (18) years shall have the right to select for himself or herself one hundred and sixty (160) acres of land to be held and owned in severalty, to conform to the legal surveys in boundary; and that the father, or, if he be dead, the mother, if members of either of said tribes of Indians, shall have the right to select a like amount of land for each of his or her children under the age of eighteen (18) years; and that the Commissioner of Indian Affairs, or some one by him appointed for the purpose, shall select a like amount of land for each orphan child belonging to either of said tribes under the age of eighteen (18) years.

173

ARTICLE III.

It is further agreed that the land in said reservation shall be classed as grain-growing and grazing land; and in making selection of lands to be allotted in severalty as aforesaid, each and every Indian, herein provided for, shall be required to take at least one-half in area, of his or her allotments, of grazing land. It is hereby further expressly agreed that no person shall have the right to make his or her selection of land in any part of said reservation that is now used or occupied for military, agency, school, school-farm, religious or other public uses or in sections sixteen (16) and thirty-six (36) in each Congressional Township; except in cases where any Commanche, Kiowa or Apache Indian has heretofore made improvements upon, and now uses and occupies a part of said sections sixteen (16) and thirty-six (36), such Indian may make his or her selection within the boundaries so prescribed so as to include his or her improvements; it is further agreed that wherever in said reservation any Indian, entitled to take lands in severalty hereunder, has made improvements, and now uses and occupies the land embracing such improvements, such Indian shall have the undisputed right to make his or her selection within the area above provided for allotments, so as to include his or her said improvements.

It is further agreed that said sections sixteen (16) and thirty-six (36) in each Congressional Township in said reservation shall not become subject to homestead entry, but shall be held by the United States and finally sold for public school purposes. It is hereby further agreed that wherever in said reservation any religious society or other organization is now occupying any portion of said reservation for religious or educational work among the Indians the land so occupied may be allotted and confirmed to such society or organization, not however to exceed one hundred and sixty (160) acres of land to any one society or organization so long as the same shall be so occupied and used; and such land shall not be subject to homestead entry.

ARTICLE IV.

All allotments hereunder shall be selected within ninety days from the ratification of this agreement by the Congress of the United States—provided the Secretary of the Interior, in his discretion, may extend the time for making such selection; and should any Indian entitled to allotments hereunder fail or refuse to make his or her selection of land in that time, then

the allotting agent in charge of the work of making such
allotments, shall within the next thirty (30) days after
said time, make allotments to such Indians, which shall
have the same force and effect as if the selection were
made by the Indian.

ARTICLE V.

When said allotments of land shall have been selected
and taken as aforesaid, and approved by the Secretary of
the Interior, the titles thereto shall be held in trust for
the allottees, respectively, for the period of twenty-five
(25) years, in the time and manner and to the extent provided for in the Act of Congress entitled: "An Act to provide for the allotment of land in severalty to Indians on
the various reservations, and to extend the protection of
the laws of the United States and Territories over the
Indians and for other purposes." Approved February 8, 1887.
And an Act amendatory thereof, approved February 28, 1891.

And at the expiration of the said period of twenty-five
(25) years the titles thereto shall be conveyed in fee simple
to the allottees, or their heirs, free from all incumbrances.

ARTICLE VI.

As a further and only additional consideration for the
cession of territory and relinquishment of title, claim and
interest in and to lands as aforesaid the United States agrees
to pay to the Commanche, Kiowa and Apache Tribes of Indians,
in the Indian Territory, the sum of two million ($2 000 000 00)
dollars, as follows; two hundred thousand ($200 000 00) dollars
in cash, to be distributed per capita, among the members of
said tribes within one hundred and twenty (120) days after
this agreement shall be ratified by the Congress of the United
States; two hundred thousand ($200 000 00) dollars to be paid
out to ~~or for~~ said Indians under the direction of the Scretary
of the Interior in one year after said first payment and one
hundred thousand ($100 000 00) dollars in the same manner in
one year from date of said second payment and the remaining
one million and five hundred thousand ($1 500 000 00) dollars
to be retained in the Treasury of the United States, placed
to the credit of said Indians, and while so retained, to draw
interest at the rate of five per centum per annum, to be paid
to the said Indians per capita annually.

Nothing herein contained shall be held to affect in any
way any annuities due said Indians under existing laws, agreements

or treaties.

Article VIII.

It is further agreed that wherever in said reservation any member of any of the tribes of said Indians has, in pursuance of any laws or under any rules or regulations of the Interior Department taken an allotment, such allotment, at the option of the allottee shall be confirmed and governed by all the conditions attached to allotments taken under this agreement.

Article IX.

It is further agreed that any and all leases, made in pursuance of the laws of the United States, of any part of said reservation which may be in force at the time of the ratification, by Congress, of this agreement shall remain in force the same as if this agreement had not been made.

Article X.

It is further agreed that the following named persons— not members by blood of either of said Tribes, but who have married into one of the tribes; to wit, Mabel R. Given, Thomas F. Woodward, William Wyatt, Kiowa Dutch, John Nestill, James N. Jones, Christian Ke-oh-tah, Edward L. Clark, George Conover, William Dietrick, Ben Roach, Lewis Bentz, Abilene, James Gardloupe, John Sanchez, the wife of Boone Chandler—whose given name is unknown, Emmit Cox and Horace P. Jones shall each be entitled to all the benefits of land and money conferred by this agreement, the same as if members by blood of one of said tribes; and that Emsy S. Smith, David Grantham, Zonee Adams, John T. Hill, J. J. Methvin, H. L. Scott, and George D. Day, friends of said Indians who have rendered to said Indians valuable services, shall each be entitled to all the benefits in land only conferred under this agreement, the same as if members of said tribes.

Article XI.

This agreement shall be effective only when ratified by the Congress of the United States.

IN WITNESS WHEREOF, we have hereunto set our hands this sixth day of October, A. D. 1892.

Said Agreement was executed on behalf of the United States and a number of the members of the petitioner tribes and duly transmitted to the President, as required by said Act of 1889.

3. Shortly after the President received said Agreement he transmitted the same to Congress for ratification, as required by the last-mentioned Act. However, Congress neglected to ratify the same, or take any action concerning it, until the 6th day of June, 1900, and on that date passed an Act entitled "An Act to ratify an agreement with the Indians of the Fort Hall Indian reservation in Idaho, and make appropriations to carry the same into effect." Section 6 of this Act (31 Stat. 672), which is the only part thereof concerning the Comanche, Kiowa, and Apache Tribes, reads as follows:

>   SEC. 6. Whereas David H. Jerome, Alfred M. Wilson, and Warren G. Sayre, duly appointed Commissioners on the part of the United States, did, on the sixth day of October, eighteen hundred and ninety-two, conclude an agreement with the Comanche, Kiowa, and Apache tribes of Indians in Oklahoma, formerly a part of the Indian Territory, which said agreement is in the words and figures as follows:
>
>   "Articles of agreement made and entered into at Fort Sill, in the Indian Territory, on the twenty-first day of October, eighteen hundred and ninety-two, by and between David H. Jerome, Alfred M. Wilson, and Warren G. Sayre, Commissioners on the part of the United States, and the Comanche, Kiowa, and Apache tribes of Indians in the Indian Territory.
>
>   "ARTICLE I.
>
>   "Subject to the allotment of land, in severalty to the individual members of the Comanche, Kiowa, and Apache tribes of Indians in the Indian Territory, as hereinafter provided for, and subject to the setting apart as grazing lands for said Indians, four hundred and eighty thousand acres of land as hereinafter provided for, and subject to the conditions hereinafter imposed, and for the considerations

hereinafter mentioned, the said Comanche, Kiowa, and Apache Indians hereby cede, convey, transfer, relinquish, and surrender, forever and absolutely, without any reservation whatever, express or implied, all their claim, title, and interest, of every kind and character, in and to the lands embraced in the following-described tract of country in the Indian Territory to wit: Commencing at a point where the Washita River crosses the ninety-eighth meridian west from Greenwich; thence up the Washita River, in the middle of the main channel thereof, to a point thirty miles, by river, west of Fort Cobb, as now established; thence due west to the north fork of Red River, provided said line strikes said river east of the one-hundredth meridian of west longitude; if not, then only to said meridian line, and thence due south, on said meridian line, to the said north fork of Red River; thence down said north fork, in the middle of the main channel thereof, from the point where it may be first intersected by the lines above described, to the main Red River; thence down said Red River, in the middle of the main channel thereof, to its intersection with the ninety-eighth meridian of longitude west from Greenwich; thence north, on said meridian line, to the place of beginning.

"ARTICLE II.

"Out of the lands ceded, conveyed, transferred, relinquished and surrendered by Article I hereof, and in part consideration for the cession thereof, it is agreed by the United States that each member of said Comanche, Kiowa, and Apache tribes of Indians over the age of eighteen (18) years shall have the right to select for himself or herself one hundred and sixty (160) acres of land to be held and owned in severalty, to conform to the legal surveys in boundary; and that the father, or, if he be dead, the mother, if members of either of said tribe of Indians, shall have the right to select a like amount of land for each of his or her children under the age of eighteen (18) years; and that the Commissioner of Indian Affairs, or some one by him appointed for the purpose, shall select a like amount of land for each orphan child belonging to either of said tribes under the age of eighteen (18) years.

"ARTICLE III.

"That in addition to the allotment of lands to said Indians as provided for in this agreement, the Secretary of the Interior shall set aside for the use in common for said Indian tribes four hundred and eighty thousand acres of grazing lands, to be selected by the Secretary of the Interior, either in one or more tracts as will best subserve the interest of said Indians. It is hereby further expressly agreed that no person shall have the right to make his or her selection of land in any part of said reservation that is now used or occupied for military, agency, school, school-farm, religious, or other public uses, or in sections sixteen (16) and thirty-six (36) in each Congressional township, except in cases where any Comanche, Kiowa, or Apache Indian has heretofore made improvements upon and now uses and occupies a part of said sections sixteen (16) and thirty-six (36), such Indian may make his or her selection within the boundaries so prescribed so as to include his or her improvements. It is further agreed that wherever in said reservation any Indian, entitled to take lands in severalty hereunder, has made improvements, and now uses and occupies the land embracing such improvements, such Indian shall have the undisputed right to make his or her selection within the area above provided for allotments, so as to include his or her said improvements.

"It is further agreed that said sections sixteen (16) and thirty-six (36) in each Congressional township in said reservation shall not become subject to homestead entry but shall be held by the United States and finally sold for public school purposes. It is hereby further agreed that wherever in said reservation any religious society or other organization is now occupying any portion of said reservation for religious or educational work among the Indians, the land so occupied may be allotted and confirmed to such society or organization, not, however, to exceed one hundred and sixty (160) acres of land to any one society or organization so long as the same shall be so occupied and used; and such land shall not be subject to homestead entry.

"ARTICLE IV.

"All allotments hereunder shall be selected within ninety days from the ratification of this agreement by the Congress of the United States: Provided, The Secretary of the Interior, in his discretion, may extend the time for making such selection; and should any Indian entitled to allotments hereunder fail or refuse to make his or her selection of land in that time, then the allotting agent in charge of the work of making such allotments shall within the next thirty (30) days after said time make allotments to such Indians, which shall have the same force and effect as if the selection were made by the Indian.

"ARTICLE V.

"When said allotments of land shall have been selected and taken as aforesaid, and approved by the Secretary of the Interior, the titles thereto shall be held in trust for the allottees, respectively, for the period of twenty-five (25) years, in the time and manner and to the extent provided for in the act of Congress entitled 'An act to provide for the allotment of land in severalty to Indians on the various reservations, and to extend the protection of the laws of the United States and Territories over the Indians, and for other purposes,' approved February 8, 1887, and an act amendatory thereof, approved February 28, 1891.

"And at the expiration of the said period of twenty-five (25) years the titles thereto shall be conveyed in fee simple to the allottees or their heirs, free from all incumbrances.

"ARTICLE VI.

"As a further and only additional consideration for the cession of territory and relinquishment of title, claim, and interest in and to the lands as aforesaid, the United States agrees to pay to the Comanche, Kiowa, and Apache tribes of Indians, in the Indian Territory, the sum of two million (2,000,000) dollars, as follows: Five hundred thousand ($500,000) dollars to be distributed per capita to the members of said tribes at such times and in such manner as the Secretary of the Interior shall deem to be for the best interests of said Indians, which sum is hereby appropriated out of any funds in the Treasury not otherwise appropriated; and any part of the same remaining unpaid shall draw interest at the rate of five per centum while remaining in the Treasury, which interest shall be paid to the Indians annually per capita; and the remaining one million five hundred thousand ($1,500,000) dollars to be retained in the Treasury of the United States, placed to the credit of said Indians, and while so retained to draw interest at the rate of five per centum per annum, to be paid to the said Indians per capita annually.

"Nothing herein contained shall be held to affect in any way annuities due said Indians under existing laws, agreements, or treaties.

"ARTICLE VIII.

"It is further agreed that wherever in said reservation

any member of any of the tribes of said Indians, has in pursuance of any laws or under any rules or regulations of the Interior Department taken an allotment, such allotment, at the option of the allottee, shall be confirmed and governed by all the conditions attached to allotments taken under this agreement.

"ARTICLE IX.

"It is further agreed that any and all leases made in pursuance of the laws of the United States of any part of said reservation which may be in force at the time of the ratification by Congress of this agreement shall remain in force the same as if this agreement had not been made.

"ARTICLE X.

"It is further agreed that the following named persons, not members by blood of either of said tribes, but who have married into one of the tribes, to wit, Mabel R. Given, Thomas F. Woodward, William Wyatt, Kiowa Dutch, John Nestill, James N. Jones, Christian Ke oh-tah, Edward L. Clark, George Conover, William Deitrick, Ben Roach, Lewis Bentz, Abilene, James Gardloupe, John Sanchez, the wife of Boone Chandler, whose given name is unknown, Emmit Cox, and Horace P. Jones, shall each be entitled to all the benefits of land and money conferred by this agreement, the same as if members by blood of one of said tribes, and that Ensy S. Smith, David Grantham, Zonee Adams, John T. Hill, and J. J. Methvin, friends of said Indians, who have rendered to said Indians valuable services, shall each be entitled to all the benefits, in land only, conferred under this agreement, the same as if members of said tribes.

"ARTICLE XI.

"This agreement shall be effective only when ratified by the Congress of the United States."

(a) Said agreement be, and the same hereby is, accepted, ratified, and confirmed as herein amended.

(b) That the Secretary of the Interior is hereby authorized and directed to cause the allotments of said lands, provided for in said treaty among said Indians, to be made by any Indian inspector or special agent.

(c) That all allotments of said land shall be made under

the direction of the Secretary of the Interior to said Indians within ninety days from the passage of this Act, subject to the exceptions contained in article four of said treaty: Provided, That the time for making allotments shall in no event be extended beyond six months from the passage of this Act.

(d) That the lands acquired by this agreement shall be opened to settlement by proclamation of the President within six months after allotments are made and be disposed of under the general provisions of the homestead and town-site laws of the United States: Provided, That in addition to the land-office fees prescribed by statute for such entries the entryman shall pay one dollar and twenty-five cents per acre for the land entered at the time of submitting his final proof: And provided further, That in all homestead entries where the entryman has resided upon and improved the land entered in good faith for the period of fourteen months he may commute his entry to cash upon the payment of one dollar and twenty-five cents per acre: And provided further, That the rights of honorably discharged Union soldiers and sailors of the late civil war, as defined and described in sections twenty-three hundred and four and twenty-three hundred and five of the Revised Statutes shall not be abridged: And provided further, That any person who, having attempted to but for any cause failed to secure a title in fee to a homestead under existing laws, or who made entry under what is known as the commuted provision of the homestead law, shall be qualified to make a homestead entry upon said lands: And provided further, That any qualified entryman having lands adjoining the lands herein ceded, whose original entry embraced less than one hundred and sixty acres in all, shall have the right to enter so much of the lands by this agreement ceded lying contiguous to his said entry as shall, with the land already entered, make in the aggregate one hundred and sixty acres, said land to be taken upon the same conditions as are required of other entrymen: And provided further, That the settlers who located on that part of said lands called and known as the "neutral strip" shall have preference right for thirty days on the lands upon which they have located and improved.

(e) That sections sixteen and thirty-six, thirteen and thirty-three, of the lands hereby acquired in each township shall not be subject to entry, but shall be reserved, sections sixteen and thirty-six for the use of the common schools, and sections thirteen and thirty-three for university, agricultural colleges, normal schools, and public buildings of the Territory and future State of Oklahoma; and in case either of said sections, or part thereof, is lost to said Territory by reason of allotment under this Act or otherwise, the governor thereof is hereby authorized to locate other lands not occupied in quantity equal to the loss.

(f) That none of the money or interest thereon which is, by the terms of the said agreement, to be paid to said Indians shall be applied to the payment of any judgment that has been or may hereafter be rendered under the provisions of the Act of Congress approved March third, eighteen hundred and ninety-one, entitled "An Act to provide for the adjudication and payment of claims arising from Indian depredations."

(g) That should any of said lands allotted to said Indians, or opened to settlement under this Act, contain valuable mineral deposits, such mineral deposits shall be open to location and entry, under the existing mining laws of the United States, upon the passage of this Act, and the mineral laws of the United States are hereby extended over said lands.

(h) That as the Choctaw and Chickasaw nations claim to have some right, title, and interest in and to the lands ceded by the foregoing treaty as soon as the same are abandoned by said Comanche, Kiowa, and Apache tribes of Indians, jurisdiction be, and is hereby conferred upon the United States Court of Claims to hear and determine the said claim of the Chickasaws and the Choctaws, and to render a judgment thereon, it being the intention of this Act to allow said Court of Claims jurisdiction, so that the rights, legal and equitable, of the United States and the Choctaw and Chickasaw nations, and the Comanche, Kiowa, and Apache tribes of Indians in the premises shall be fully considered and determined, and to try and determine all questions that may arise on behalf of either party in the hearing of said claim; and the Attorney-General is hereby directed to appear in behalf of the Government of the United States; and either of the parties to said action shall have the right to appeal to the Supreme Court of the United States: Provided, That such appeal shall be taken within sixty days after the rendition of the judgment objected to, and that the said courts shall give such causes precedence: And provided further, That nothing in this Act shall be accepted or construed as a confession that the United States admit that the Choctaw and Chickasaw nations have any claim to or interest in said lands or any part thereof.

(i) That said action shall be presented by a single

- 14 -

petition making the United States party defendant, and shall set forth all the facts on which the said Choctaw and Chickasaw nations claim title to said land; and said petition may be verified by the authorized delegates, agents, or attorneys of said Indians upon their information and belief as to the existence of such facts, and no other statement or verification shall be necessary: <u>Provided</u>, That if said Choctaw and Chickasaw nations do not bring their action within ninety days from the approval of this Act, or should they dismiss said suit, and the same shall not be reinstated, their claim shall be forever barred: <u>And provided further,</u> That, in the event it shall be adjudged in the final judgment or decree rendered in said action that said Choctaw and Chickasaw Nations have any right, title, or interest in or to said lands for which they should be compensated by the United States, then said sum of one million five hundred thousand ($1,500,000) dollars, shall be subject to such legislation as Congress may deem proper.

Approved, June 6, 1900.

The lettering of the paragraphs shown above does not appear in the original Act but is added as a convenience for reference in these findings and in the opinion of the Commission.

184

4. By the Act of June 6, 1900, the defendant acquired ~~2,968,893~~ 2,991,933 acres of land, out of which, and in accordance with the provisions of said Act, it set apart as grazing lands for said Indians 480,000 acres (100,000 acres of these pasture lands were later allotted to individual members of said tribes). The defendant also allotted, in severalty, to the individual members of said tribes 445,000 acres out of lands other than the pasture lands referred to above; so, there were actually allotted in severalty to said Indians 545,000 acres of the lands acquired by the defendant under said Act. In addition, the defendant set aside 10,310 acres for agency, school, religious, and

other purposes. After the disposition of the lands acquired as above set forth, the balance of the area acquired by the defendant comprised 2,033,583 acres, for which balance the defendant eventually paid the petitioners the sum of $2,000,000, which sum was either distributed to or placed to the credit of petitioners in the Treasury of the United States.

5. So what defendant actually acquired under the Act of 1900 was 2,033,583 acres of land free of Indian title, and of this area the defendant granted 225,953 acres to Oklahoma for educational purposes and sold the remaining 1,807,630 acres to entrymen under the Public Land Laws of the United States. No part of the proceeds derived from the sales of this land were paid to or credited to petitioners.

BEFORE THE INDIAN CLAIMS COMMISSION

THE KIOWA, COMANCHE AND)
APACHE TRIBES OF INDIANS,)
)
   Petitioners,)
)
  v.   ) Docket No. 32
)
THE UNITED STATES OF AMERICA,)
)
   Defendant.)

Appearances:

  W. C. Lewis, J. Roy Thompson, Jr.
  and Frank Miskovsky,
  Attorneys for Petitioners.

  Ralph A. Barney, with whom was
  Mr. Assistant Attorney General
  A. Devitt Vanech,
  Attorneys for Defendant.

April 9, 1951

OPINION OF THE COMMISSION

O'Marr, Associate Commissioner, delivered the opinion of the Commission.

1. The Claim here asserted by the petitioners, the Kiowa, Comanche, and Apache Tribes of Indians, is to recover the sum of $16,268,664 less $2,000,000 paid by the Government, for 2,033,583 acres of land lying west of the 98th Meridian in what is now the State of Oklahoma, which land is part of an area of 2,968,893 acres situated in a larger territory historically known as the Leased District.

2. The lands involved in this case were acquired by the petitioners under the Treaty of October 21, 1867, 15 Stat. 581. By this

treaty the land hereinafter described were ceded by the United States to the Confederated Tribes of Kiowa and Comanche Indians; that the lands so ceded are located in the State of Oklahoma and are described in the treaty as follows:

> "commencing at a point where the Washita River crosses the 98th meridian, west from Geeenwich; thence up the Washita River, in the middle of the main channel thereof, to a point thirty miles, by river, west of Fort Cobb, as now established; thence, due west to the north fork of Red River, provided said line strikes said river east of the one hundredth meridian of west longitude; if not, then only to said meridian-line, and thence south, on said meridian-line, to the said north fork of Red River; thence down said north fork, in the middle of the main channel thereof, from the point where it may be first intersected by the lines above described, to the main Red River; thence down said river, in the middle of the main channel thereof to its intersection with the ninety-eighth meridian of longitude west from Greenwich; thence north, on said meridian-line, to the place of beginning, * * *." (Finding No. 1)

Subsequent to said cession, and on the same day that said treaty was executed, the said Apache Tribe of Indians united with the Kiowa and Comanche Tribes, and thereafter shared and enjoyed jointly with the Kiowa and Comanche Tribes all the above-described land and the benefits arising from said treaty. See treaty between the United States and the Kiowa, Comanche and Apache Tribes of Indians, dated October 21, 1867, and ratified July 25, 1868, 15 Stat. 589. Said treaty with the Kiowa and Comanche is historically known as the Medicine Lodge Treaty.

3. Pursuant to section 14 of the Act of March 2, 1889, 25 Stat. 980, the President of the United States appointed a Commis-

sion, composed of David H. Jerome, Chairman, Warren G. Sayre and Alfred M. Wilson, to negotiate an agreement with petitioners for the cession of their lands in the ceded area, and said Commissioner on the 6th day of October, 1892 (this date is sometimes referred to as the 21st day of October, 1892), concluded an agreement by which the petitioners ceded all of their lands described in paragraph 2 hereof, to the United States, and the United States agreed to allot to each member of the petitioner tribes, over the age of 18 years, 160 acres of the lands ceded, and the members of said tribes were also allowed to select a like area for each of his or her children under the age of 18 years. A copy of said agreement so negotiated and concluded appears in Finding No. 2 hereof and is historically known as the Jerome Agreement, and will be so referred to hereafter, or as "the agreement."

The agreement contained an express provision that it should become effective only when ratified by the Congress of the United States.

4. On the 22d day of October, 1892, the Commissioners who negotiated the Jerome Agreement transmitted the same to the President. In due time the President reported said agreement to the Congress; however, Congress took no action thereon until it passed the Act of June 6, 1900, 31 Stat. 677. A copy of said Act, insofar as it applies to the matter here under consideration, is set forth in Finding No. 3 hereof, being Section 6 of said Act; that by said Act the Congress did not ratify the Jerome Agreement in the form in which it was negotiated

and submitted to it by the President, but made substantial changes therein, which will be hereinafter referred to.

5. After the passage of said Act of June 6, 1900, purporting to ratify the Jerome Agreement, the so-called ratified agreement was not submitted to the petitioners for their consideration and approval of the changes made by Congress in said Act of 1900, nor was said Act, as passed by Congress, ever submitted to petitioners for their consideration or approval, nor have petitioners ever approved the same, although the $2,000,000 provided for in Article VI of the agreement appearing in said Act of 1900 was eventually paid as required by the provisions of said Article. (Finding No. 4).

6. As required by the Act of June 6, 1900, the defendant made individual allotments to the members of the three tribes in the aggregate amount of 445,000 acres and set apart 480,000 acres of pasture land for the common use of said Indians; however, 100,000 acres of this pasture land was later allotted to individual members of said tribes. The defendant also set apart for agency, school, religious, and other purposes, 10,310 acres. So there remained the 2,033,583 acres which the defendant received under the Act and which is the land involved in this claim. (See Finding No. 4).

7. Let us now compare the provisions of the Jerome Agreement, which was executed by the treaty Commissioners and the Indians in 1892, with the provisions of the Act of 1900. In the Act of June 6, 1900,

31 Stat. 677, which purports to ratify the Jerome Agreement, we find in Article I that the cession of the 2,968,893 acres was subject to the allotments to the individual Indians and subject to setting apart as grazing lands for said Indians 480,000 acres of land for grazing purposes. No mention of the reserve for grazing purposes was made in the Jerome Agreement, and in Article III of the so-called ratified agreement provision is made for the setting aside of the grazing land by the Secretary of the Interior for use in common by said Indians. There is no provision of that character in the Jerome Agreement.

Article VI of the Jerome Agreement provided for the payment to the petitioners the sum of $2,000,000 as follows: $200,000 in cash to be distributed per capita within 120 days after the ratification of the agreement; $200,000 to be paid out for the Indians under the direction of the Secretary of the Interior, and $100,000 to be paid in the same manner within one year from the date of the second payment, and the remaining $1,500,000 to be retained in the Treasury of the United States to the credit of the Indians and to draw interest at the rate of five per centum per annum, the interest to be distributed to the Indians per capita each year. In the purported ratification of the agreement, Article VI was changed to provide for the payment of said $2,000,000 as follows: $500,000 to be distributed per capita to the members of said tribes in such manner as the Secretary of the Interior shall deem to be for the best interests of the Indians, and the balance of the payment to be credited to the Indians and the interest thereon distributed as provided in the Jerome Agreement. Thus, it will be seem that a substantial change was made in the terms of payment; but that was not all; for in the last paragraph of the Act of June 6, 1900 /Finding 3 (i)/ the payment of the $1,500,000 is required to be held until an alleged claim of title to said land by the Choctaw and Chickasaw Nations had been determined, and in the event that it should be adjudged in any suit brought by the Choctaw and Chickasaw Nations, as authorized by said Act of June 6, 1900 that they have any compensable right in said lands, the payment of said sum of $1,500,000 shall be subject to such legislation as Congress may deem proper. No such condition or contingency as this appears in the Jerome Agreement.

Again, the Jerome Agreement, by Article III, reserved sections 16 and 36 in each township for public school purposes, and such school lands may not be selected for allotments unless occupied by Indians. This provision was not substantially changed in the ratified agreement. However, in the legislative portion of the Act of 1900 following the purported ratification of the agreement /Finding 3 (e)/, it is provided that in addition to sections 16 and 36 in each township of the cession which shall be reserved for use of the common schools, sections 13 and 33 in each township were reserved for the university, agricultural collages, normal schools, and public buildings of the Territory and fugure State of Oklahoma, and in the event that a part of the reserved sections should be occupied, land in lieu thereof might be selected. Sections 13 and 33 were not reserved by any provision of the Jerome

Agreement, or for that matter, by any provision of the agreement ratified by the Act of 1900. The reservation of sections 13 and 33 would perhaps not affect the Indians unless they were not subject to allotment.

Furthermore, and contrary to the Jerome Agreement, it is provided in the legislative portion of said Act that the lands allotted to the Indians, which may contain valuable mineral deposits, such deposits shall be open to location and entry under the then existing mineral laws of the United States, which were extended to cover the said lands. /Finding 3 (g)/.

And furthermore, by Article III of the Jerome Agreement provision was made for the classification of the lands to be allotted into grain-growing and grazing land, and the allottes were required to select at least half of their allotment in grazing land. This provision was entirely eliminated from the agreement set forth in the 1900 Act.

8. From the foregoing it will be seen that there were not only substantial changes made in the Jerome Agreement as it was acted upon by Congress, but the legislative provisions following the purported ratification in the Act of 1900 added further conditions and restrictions to the plan agreed to by the Indians and the Commissioners appointed to negotiate the agreement, and, as we have stated before, the new plan or arrangement adopted by Congress in said Act was never submitted to the Indians for their acceptance or approval, and was never agreed to by them.

9. The appointment of Commissioners to negotiate an agreement with the petitioners for the government's acquisition of their lands, and the Jerome Agreement consummated with the Indians, in truth and in fact amounted to nothing more than an offer by the Indians to cede their lands for the consideration and upon the terms and conditions set forth in the Jerome Agreement, because any agreement that might be entered into was subject to the approval of Congress, not only by the express provisions of section 14 of the Act of March 2, 1889, 25 Stat. 980, but by the express provisions of the Jerome Agreement itself.

10. It is elementary law that when an offer is made, as was done here by the Jerome Agreement, the acceptance of it must be substantially as made, and there must be no variation between the acceptance and the offer. In other words, the acceptance must be without substantial qualification, condition, or departure from the offer. 12 Am. Jur., p. 543, sec. 53; Iselin v. United States, 271 U. S. 136, 70 L. Ed. 872; Minneapolis etc. v. Columbus, 119 U. S. 149, 30 L. Ed. 376; First National Bank v. Hall, 101 U. S. 50, 25 L. Ed. 822.

11. It is plain from the above that the passage of the 1900 Act created no contractual obligations on the part of petitioners for the Jerome Agreement was substantially changed by Congress, not only by the changes of its terms and the addition of new clauses, but by legislatively imposing conditions and restrictions which affected the

Indian selection and enjoyment of their allotments and the payment of
the purchase price. Accordingly, Congress ignored the offer of the
petitioners to sell in the manner and upon the conditions set forth
in the Jerome Agreement, and by virtue of said Act the Government
acquired the land without the consent of the Indians upon its own
terms and conditions and in disregard of the rights of the Indians
under the treaty of October 21, 1867. That the Government had this
power no one can deny. Lone Wolf v. United States, 187 U. S. 553,
47 L. Ed. 299. However, by exercising the power it had does not relieve defendant from paying the Indians any damages they may have sustained through such action.

12. Because of the above, it is not necessary to determine
whether the imoperative Jerome Agreement was obtained by fraud, duress,
mistake, or based upon an unconscionable consideration, or whether the
number of Indians, required by Article 12 of the 1867 treaty, executed
it.

13. So, we reach the conclusion that under our rules of procedure
/Sec. 22 (f)/ the petitioners have sustained the issue of fact and law
relating to their right to recover; however, since an award is dependent
upon the difference, if any, between the value of the land at the time
it was acquired by the defendant and the amount paid, less allowable
offsets, that question can only be determined upon a final hearing of
the claim. Our order will now be, therefore, that the case proceed
for the purpose of determining the difference, if any, between the

value of the land of June 6, 1900, and the purchase price paid petitioners, and the amount of offsets, if any, the defendant may be entitled to.

Chief Commissioner Witt and Associate Commissioner Holt concur.

April 9, 1951

26 Ind. Cl. Comm. 101

BEFORE THE INDIAN CLAIMS COMMISSION

THE KIOWA, COMANCHE AND APACHE)
  TRIBES OF INDIANS,)
)
             Plaintiffs,)
)
THE WICHITA INDIAN TRIBE OF OKLAHOMA)
  AND BANDS AND GROUPS OF INDIANS)
  WHICH HAVE BEEN OR WHICH ARE AFFIL-)
  IATED WITH THE WICHITA INDIAN TRIBE)
  OF OKLAHOMA, INCLUDING BUT NOT LIM-)
  ITED TO THE WICHITA, WACOS, KEECHIS,)
  AND TOWACONIES,)
)
           Plaintiffs and) Docket No. 257
            Intervenors,)
)
     v.)
)
THE UNITED STATES OF AMERICA,)
)
            Defendant.)

Decided: August 9, 1971

Appearances:

    J. Roy Thompson, Jr., Attorney for The Kiowa,
    Comanche and Apache Tribes of Indians,
    Plaintiffs.

    Omer Luellen, with whom was Paul M. Niebell,
    Attorneys for The Wichita Indian Tribe of
    Oklahoma and Affiliated Bands and Groups.

    Bernard M. Sisson, with whom was Mr. Assistant
    Attorney General Shiro Kashiwa, Attorneys for
    the Defendant.

OPINION ON MOTION OF THE KIOWA, COMANCHE AND
APACHE TRIBES OF INDIANS FOR
SUMMARY JUDGMENT OF RECOGNIZED TITLE
AND DEFENDANT'S ALTERNATIVE MOTION
TO DISMISS CLAIM FOR FAILURE TO PROSECUTE

Commissioner Yarborough delivered the opinion of the Commission.

The Commission now has before it for decision the motion of the Kiowa, Comanche and Apache Tribes, plaintiffs, for summary judgment in which the Commission is asked to determine summarily as a matter of law that, by virtue of the Treaty of October 18, 1865, between the United States and the Kiowa and Comanche Tribes of Indians, 14 Stat. 717, ratified May 22, 1866, and proclaimed May 26, 1866, the Kiowa, Comanche and Apache Tribes of Indians acquired recognized title to the tract of land described by metes and bounds in Article II thereof, 14 Stat. 718. The tract consists of approximately 39,680,000 acres located in the northwestern part of the present State of Texas and the western portion of the present State of Oklahoma, and officially designated Areas 510 and 511 on Map 57, Texas and Portions of Adjoining States, in Part II of the 18th Annual Report of the Bureau of American Ethnology, 1896-1897 (hereinafter referred to as Royce Areas 510 and 511).

In responding to the Kiowa motion, the defendant insists that there are genuine issues of material fact which must be decided before the Commission can resolve the recognized title question and, since defendant has raised such genuine issues of material fact, the motion for summary judgment must be denied. The defendant further urges that this issue is _res judicata_ in that the plaintiffs previously moved the Commission to grant an identical motion for summary judgment

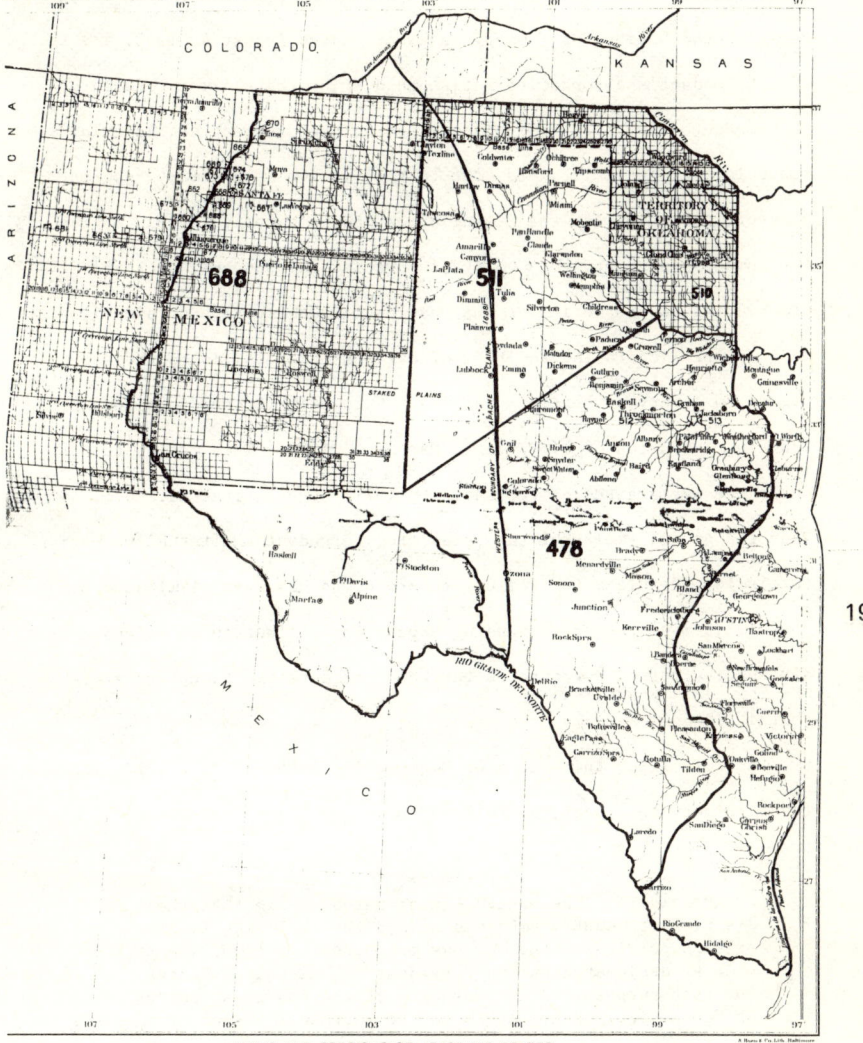

TEXAS AND PORTIONS OF ADJOINING STATES
SCALE 80 MILES TO 1 INCH

of recognized title and said motion was denied. See Order Overruling Petitioners' Motion For Summary Judgment, dated August 4, 1960.

Defendant's alternative motion to dismiss the claim for failure to prosecute was based upon an anticipated postponement of the trial scheduled for April 13, 1970, due to this motion for summary judgment. However, subsequent to the filing of defendant's reply to this motion for summary judgment, the Commission ordered the suspension of all proceedings on the merits of the case pending a decision on a motion made by the Wichita Indian Tribe of Oklahoma and Affiliated Bands and Groups to intervene herein. See Order Suspending Proceedings and Granting Extension of Time, dated March 25, 1970. This motion to intervene was granted on February 10, 1971. See 24 Ind. Cl. Comm. 405. Thus the ground (delay of the trial) for defendant's alternative motion to dismiss the claim for failure to prosecute has been eliminated by the Commission's order suspending proceedings. Therefore, defendant's alternative motion warrants no further consideration except to state that it is denied.

Article II of the Treaty of October 18, 1865, 14 Stat. 717, 718, reads, in pertinent part, as follows:

* * *

> Article II. The United States hereby agree that the district of country embraced within the following limits, or such portion of the same as may hereafter from time to time be designated by the President of the United States for that purpose, viz: commencing at the northeast corner of New Mexico, thence south to the southeast corner of

the same; thence northeastwardly to a point on main Red river opposite the mouth of the North Fork of said river; thence down said river to the 98th degree of west longitude; thence due north on said meridian to the Cimarone river; thence up said river to a point where the same crosses the southern boundary of the State of Kansas; thence along said southern boundary of Kansas to the southwest corner of said State; thence west to the place of beginning, shall be and is hereby set apart for the absolute and undisturbed use and occupation of the tribes who are parties to this treaty, and of such other friendly tribes as have heretofore resided within said limits, or as they may from time to time agree to admit among them, and that no white person except officers, agents, and employes of the government shall go upon or settle within the country embraced within said limits, unless formally admitted and incorporated into some one of the tribes lawfully residing there, according to its laws and usages. The Indians parties hereto on their part expressly agree to remove to and accept as their permanent home the country embraced within said limits, whenever directed so to do by the President of the United States, in accordance with the provisions of this treaty, * * * and that henceforth they will and do hereby relinquish all claims or rights in and to any portion of the United States or territories, except such as is embraced within the limits aforesaid, and more especially their claims and rights in and to the country north of the Cimarone river and west of the eastern boundary of New Mexico.

* * *

Two years later, the Kiowa and Comanche Tribes entered into another treaty with the United States whereby there was reserved "for the absolute and undisturbed use and occupation" of said tribes a portion of the tract set aside by the previous treaty consisting of approximately 3,000,000 acres in Indian Territory (Royce Area 510). The Treaty of October 21, 1867, 15 Stat. 581, ratified July 25, 1868, and proclaimed August 25, 1868, also provided for the discontinuance of all annuities under the 1865 Treaty and the substitution of annuities and items of clothing described in the 1867 Treaty. The Kiowa and Comanche Tribes agreed to relinquish all right to occupy permanently the territory outside the reservation created by the 1867 Treaty and agreed to make this new reservation their permanent home.

The rights of the Kiowa-Apache Band under the Treaty of October 18, 1865, supra, between the United States and the Kiowa and Comanche Tribes depend upon a second treaty of October 21, 1867, 15 Stat. 589, ratified July 25, 1868, and proclaimed August 25, 1868, between the United States and the Kiowa and Comanche Tribes and the Kiowa-Apache Band. Under this treaty it was agreed that this Apache band would confederate with the Kiowa and Comanche Tribes and would accept as their permanent home the reservation (Royce Area 510) described in Article II of the Treaty of October 21, 1867, supra, at 582, between the United States and the Kiowa and Comanche Tribes.

Both of these 1867 treaties were negotiated by the Indian Peace Commission, a body established by act of Congress:

> *** to call together the chiefs and headmen of such bands or tribes of Indians as are now waging war against the United States or committing depredations upon the people thereof, to ascertain the alleged reasons for their acts of hostility, and in their discretion, under the direction of the President, to make and conclude with said bands or tribes such treaty stipulations, subject to the action of the Senate, as may remove all just causes of complaint on their part, and at the same time establish security for person and property along the lines of railroad now being constructed to the Pacific and other thoroughfares of travel to the western Territories, and such as will most likely insure civilization for the Indians and peace and safety for the whites. (Act of July 20, 1867, 15 Stat. 17)

The statute further gave these commissioners the authority to select areas for permanent reservations for all the tribes treated with, subject to the approval of the Senate.

Plaintiffs' principal claim in this suit is that the 1867 Treaty took from them without the payment of adequate consideration the lands, consisting of Royce Area 511, in which they had recognized title by virtue of the 1865 Treaty. Plaintiffs have also asserted an alternative claim of aboriginal ownership of approximately 100 million acres in southwestern Kansas, southeastern Colorado, eastern New Mexico, northern Texas, and the western portion of Oklahoma, being Royce Areas 478, 510 and 511, Map 57, Texas. However, plaintiffs have stated that they do not intend to pursue this claim should they prevail on this motion for summary judgment of recognized title to Royce Areas 510 and 511.

In proceedings before the Indian Claims Commission summary judgment " *** shall be rendered if the pleadings, depositions, and admissions on file, together with the affidavits, if any, show that there is no genuine issue as to any material fact and that the moving party is entitled to a judgment as a matter of law. A summary judgment may be rendered on the issue of liability alone although there is a genuine issue as to the amount of damages." Indian Claims Commission General Rules of Procedure, 25 C.F.R. §503.11(c)(1)(iii) (1969).

The denial of a motion for summary judgment is not res judicata. In the interest of effective judicial administration, a prior denial

of a motion for summary judgment may be departed from if good reason
is shown why the prior ruling is no longer applicable or should
otherwise be disregarded. Dictograph Products Company, Inc. v.
Sonotone Corporation, 230 F.2d 131, rehearing denied, 231 F.2d 867,
petition for cert. dismissed, 352 U.S. 883 (1956); 6 Moore's Federal
Practice §56.14[2] (1966). Here, formerly disputed issues of material
fact have been resolved in other proceedings before the Commission
since the 1960 denial, and we shall consider the motion on the merits.

The first issue alleged by the United States to be a genuine
issue of material fact is that the Treaty of October 21, 1867, supra,
with the Kiowa and Comanche Tribes was the equivalent of a Presidential
designation of a lesser area as a reservation, such a designation
having been authorized in Article II of the 1865 Treaty by the
words "or such portion of the same as may hereafter from time to time
be designated by the President of the United States for that purpose."
This is, however, a legal issue involving the interpretation of the
two treaties rather than an issue of fact. Citizen Band of Potawatomi
Indians of Oklahoma v. United States, 179 Ct. Cl. 473, 482, 391 F.2d 614,
618 (1967), cert. denied 389 U.S. 1046 (1968).

The proceedings leading to the 1865 Treaty make no reference to
the inclusion of this clause in the treaty. The Indians were told
only that the United States proposed "to give for a reservation the
following described territory, from which white men will be prohibited

from entering except on permission from your agent." See Plaintiffs' Exhibit B in support of motion, App. B9. The proceedings leading to the 1867 Treaty (plaintiffs' Exhibit C) and other documents relating to that treaty (List of Documents Concerning the Negotiation of Ratified Indian Treaties 1801-1869, Special List No. 6, National Archives, 158-160 (1949)) do not reveal any intention by the United States to consider the 1867 Treaty as an implementation of the clause in the 1865 Treaty granting the President power to designate a smaller reservation.

The communication dated January 8, 1866, from the Commissioner of Indian Affairs to the Secretary of the Interior transmitting the Treaty of October 18, 1865, and the Annual Report of the Commissioner of Indian Affairs for the Year 1866 were not part of the record in this case. The Commission, however, has found these documents to be relevant and material on the question of interpretation of the two treaties and has, this day, entered an order admitting portions of these documents in evidence as Commission Exhibits 1 and 2, respectively.

The communication dated January 8, 1866, from the Commissioner of Indian Affairs to the Secretary discusses the 1865 Treaty at some length as follows:

* * *

Third. As to the treaty with the Kiowas and Comanches. It will be observed, in regard to this treaty, that it does not undertake to limit the Indians to any small reservation,

205

but includes a very large district of country, comprising about 62000 square miles, which they are to be allowed to have 'absolute and undisturbed use and occupation,' ie; the tribes treated with, and 'such as they may agree to admit among them.' This vast region, thus set apart, may be limited at the discretion of the President. As described in the treaty, it does not contain any land over which the Government has absolute control, being owned and claimed by the state of Texas, the Cherokees, Creeks, Seminoles and Choctaws and Chickasaws. Of a portion of it, however, the Government has a perpetual lease, for the occupation of certain small tribes or bands of Indians. The Commissioners evidently had in view the contemplated arrangement with the Southern Indians, in making this treaty with the Kiowas and Comanches, and expected that the western portions of the Indian country would be placed at the disposal of the Government, but they evidently overlooked the fact that more than one half of the region set apart for these tribes belongs to the state of Texas. Of course this treaty, for this reason alone, requires amendment, unless, indeed, it might, on consideration by the Senate be deemed advisable and practicable to obtain a cession of the country in question from Texas.

The treaty, in effect, amounts to a permission to the Indians to remain in any portion of the country where they have hitherto ranged, except that part lying in Kansas, Colorado, and New Mexico, though it allows them to range, for the present, the country south of the Arkansas, and they are to receive annuities in the amount of $10 per capita until they settle upon a limited reservation, and $15 per capita after that time. * * * (Commission Exhibit 1: National Archives, Office of Indian Affairs, Record Group No. 75, Report Books, Vol. 15, pp. 26-30)

The Annual Report of the Commissioner of Indian Affairs for the Year 1866 followed the above letter by several months. In this report, apparent reference is made to the provision under consideration in Article II of the 1865 Treaty in the following terms:

* * * They [the Kiowas and Comanches] were induced to come in to the appointed rendezvous on the Little Arkansas, in October, 1865, and there agreed to the terms of a treaty, by which they were to yield all claim to occupancy of any

land in Kansas, New Mexico, or Colorado, and assigned, as a range of country in which to obtain their subsistence by the chase until a permanent reservation should be given to them, a wide district lying in northwestern Texas and the Indian country. * * * As the district assigned to these Indians is all in Texas or the Indian country, special arrangements must be eventually made with the parties owning the lands, when these tribes are required to concentrate in one locality.

* * *

(Commission Exhibit 2: Annual Report of the Commissioner of Indian Affairs to the Secretary of the Interior for the Year 1866, pp.3-4)

Treaties with the Cheyenne and Arapahoe Tribes were negotiated at the same time and by the same treaty commissioners as the 1865 and 1867 treaties with the Kiowa and Comanche Tribes. In the Treaty of October 14, 1865, with the Cheyenne and Arapahoe Tribes, 14 Stat. 703, 704, there appeared language similar to that in the 1865 Treaty with the Kiowa and Comanche Tribes, including a clause granting the President authority to designate a portion of the area described in the treaty as a reservation. The area described in the treaty was located in Kansas and Indian Territory adjacent to the area described in the 1865 Treaty with the Kiowas and Comanches. However, in ratifying the 1865 Treaty with the Cheyenne and Arapahoe Tribes on May 22, 1866 (the same day the treaty with the Kiowas and Comanches was ratified), the Senate amended the treaty to provide that "* * * as soon as practicable, with the consent of said tribes, the President of the United States shall designate for said tribes a reservation, no part of which shall be within the State of Kansas * * *." This amendment was approved by the Cheyenne and Arapahoe Tribes on November 10, 1866, and had the effect of replacing the language of the treaty which was similar to that in the 1865 Treaty with the Kiowa and Comanche Tribes. The Treaty of October 28, 1867, with the Cheyenne and Arapahoe Indians, 15 Stat. 593, ratified July 25, 1868, and proclaimed August 19, 1868, set aside a smaller area in Indian Territory "for the absolute and undisturbed use and occupation" of the Cheyenne and Arapahoe Tribes. The tribes were dissatisfied with this reservation and asked for a different location. By the Executive Order of August 10, 1869, I Kapp. 839, another area in Indian Territory was set aside which the tribes occupied. The Commission, in Cheyenne and Arapahoe Tribes v. United States, 10 Ind. Cl. Comm. 1, 35-37 (1961) found that the 1867 Treaty and the 1869 Executive Order were intended to satisfy the promise, created by the amendment to the 1865 Treaty, of a reservation for the tribes. It was only because of the Senate amendment requiring the President to act that the 1867 Treaty was found to implement the earlier treaty. In the case of the 1865 Treaty with the Kiowas and Comanches the language permitted the President to act in his discretion and there was no amendment. Thus, there is no analogy between the cases.

Our analysis of the two treaties with the Kiowas and Comanches and the related documents leads us to the conclusion that the 1867 Treaty was not intended to constitute implementation of that clause in the 1865 Treaty permitting the President to designate a smaller area as a reservation. We interpret that clause in the 1865 Treaty as granting the President power to establish such a smaller reservation by Executive order if, at some indefinite future time, the circumstances might, in his discretion, require such action. This was never done. Congress chose, by the Act of July 20, 1867, supra, to treat with several of the western tribes, including the Kiowas, Comanches and Kiowa-Apaches, in order to stabilize the western frontier. In choosing so to do, Congress was apparently willing to acknowledge the plaintiffs' rights in the lands reserved by the 1865 Treaty because under the 1867 Treaty Congress ratified the cession of these lands to the United States. The Court of Claims, in considering a similar situation has stated:

* * *

> The defendant contends, as it did in the original case, that the Indian title to the 87,000 acres was not permanent or exclusive, merely a right to occupy the lands, and subject to termination by certain articles of the treaty of 1864. It is asserted that inasmuch as the treaty provisions set aside the delimited reservation to plaintiff Indians, they to occupy the same 'until otherwise directed by the President of the United States', the act of Congress taking the 87,000 acres was an exercise of this power.
>
> We cannot assent to the proposition. The President did not exercise any such power if he possessed it. On the contrary, Congress recognized the Indians' right to the lands and sought to pay for them. * * * (Klamath Indians v. United States, 85 Ct. Cl. 451, 463-464 (1937), aff'd. 304 U.S. 119 (1938))

The case of <u>Yankton Sioux Tribe</u> v. <u>United States</u>, 22 Ind. Cl. Comm. 344 (1969), is clearly distinguishable in that there the Government knew in negotiating the Treaty of April 19, 1858, 11 Stat. 742, that the lands involved were disputed among the Indians and the alleged words of recognition in the treaty were unclear and ambiguous, 22 Ind. Cl. Comm. 349-350.

We have based our interpretation both on the statutory origin of the 1867 Kiowa-Comanche Treaty and on the absence, in the treaty and in the documents supporting it, of any evidence of intent to rely upon the earlier treaty in reducing the boundaries established by said earlier treaty. We believe this interpretation to be consistent with the accepted standard of interpreting Indian treaties. See <u>United States v. Shoshone Indians</u>, 304 U.S. 111, 116 (1938).

The United States further urges, as a genuine issue of material fact, breach of the 1865 Treaty by the Indians through the commission of depredations against whites between 1865 and 1867. The defendant, however, has not denied that the United States made the annuity payments required by the 1865 Treaty during the period it now alleges the Indians breached the treaty. Furthermore, the 1867 Treaty contains a provision (Article X) releasing the United States from further payments under the 1865 Treaty and substituting therefor annuities and provisions described in Article X of the 1867 Treaty. In view of these facts, not disputed by defendant, we do not believe that defendant's bare allegation of breach of the 1865 Treaty creates a genuine issue of material fact in this case.

Lastly, defendant has alleged as a genuine issue of material fact that other tribes had rights to certain of the lands within the area described in the 1865 Treaty in derogation of the rights therein of the Kiowa, Comanche and Apache Tribes. On the one hand, the defendant points to the language in Article II of the 1865 Treaty setting apart the reservation for the Kiowa and Comanche Tribes and "such other friendly tribes as have heretofore resided within said limits." On the other hand, the defendant alleges that other tribes had title to some of these lands by virtue of prior treaties with the United States. The defendant insists that the identification of these tribes and their interests involves genuine issues of material fact which can only be resolved by trial.

The lands wherein the defendant alleges that other tribes had interests are certain areas in what is now the State of Oklahoma, west of the north-south line formed by longitude 98° west and the Cimarron River. This line is the eastern boundary of the plaintiffs' recognized title claim. The defendant alleges no such rights in other tribes to the Texas lands. The Government defends against plaintiffs' claim of recognized title to these Texas lands on other grounds which we shall discuss later in this opinion.

There has been a significant amount of litigation involving the Oklahoma lands. Certain conclusions arrived at in these suits are relevant to a proper disposition of the title questions presented in this motion for summary judgment, and determine those questions as a matter of law. In the case of Choctaw and Chickasaw Nations v. United States, 34 Ct. Cl. 17 (1899), rev'd. 179 U.S. 494 (1900), to which the Wichita Tribe and Affiliated Bands were parties, the Court of Claims found that by the Treaty of June 22, 1855, 11 Stat. 611, between the United States and the Choctaw and Chickasaw Nations all Choctaw and Chickasaw claims to lands west of longitude 100° west were relinquished to the United States; that the Choctaws and Chickasaws leased in perpetuity their lands between longitudes 98° west and 100° west to the United States for the permanent settlement of the Wichita Tribe and certain other tribes or bands of Indians; that the Wichitas and certain affiliated bands were settled in 1859 on a tract located within the leased district; and, that the Treaty of April 28, 1866, 14 Stat. 769, between the United States and the Choctaw and Chickasaw Nations did not absolutely divest these tribes of their interests in the leased district. The Supreme Court, at 179 U.S. 494, supra, reversed the Court of Claims with respect to the latter point, holding that the leased district was ceded absolutely to the United States by the Treaty of April 28, 1866. The Leased District is Area 485 on Royce's Map 2 of Indian Territory and Oklahoma.

By the Treaty of July 19, 1866, 14 Stat. 799, the Cherokee Nation authorized the United States to settle friendly tribes on the Cherokee Outlet (Royce Area 489, the northern portion of the present State of Oklahoma from longitude 98° west to longitude 100° west).

In the case of Cherokee Nation v. United States, 9 Ind. Cl. Comm. 162, 216-217 (1961), the Commission held that the Cherokee Nation retained a fee interest in the Outlet until other tribes were actually settled there.

The remaining tracts within Royce Area 511 wherein the defendant has alleged that other tribes had rights are those portions of Royce Area 480 (which includes the area separately denominated Royce Area 404) and Royce Area 486 which are west of longitude 98° west (Map 2 of Indian Territory and Oklahoma). Royce Area 480 was ceded to the United States by the Seminole Nation in the Treaty of March 21, 1866, 14 Stat. 755. The Creek Nation ceded Royce Area 486 to the United States by the Treaty of June 14, 1866, 14 Stat. 785.

We have also observed that in the above-quoted letter, dated January 8, 1866, from the Commissioner of Indian Affairs forwarding the 1865 Treaty to the Secretary of the Interior (Commission Exhibit 1), the Commissioner stated that the area reserved was "owned and claimed by the state of Texas, the Cherokees, Creeks, Seminoles and Choctaws and Chickasaws." He stated further that, with regard to a portion of the reserved area "the Government has a perpetual lease, for the occupation of certain small tribes or bands of Indians." His letter also states that the Treaty Commissioners "evidently had in view the contemplated arrangement with the Southern Indians, ***, and expected that the western portions of the Indian country would be placed at the disposal of the Government." This obviously refers to the series of 1866 treaties with the Five Civilized Tribes.

Thus the Commission may take notice that at the time of the Treaty of October 18, 1865, supra, with the Kiowa and Comanche Tribes, the Choctaw and Chickasaw Nations, the Creek Nation, the Seminole Nation and the Cherokee Nation all had title to lands located within the Oklahoma portion of Royce Area 511 and the Wichitas and affiliated bands were occupying the tract within the Oklahoma portion of Royce Area 511 upon which they had been permanently settled by the United States in 1859. We further note that during the period the 1865 Treaty was pending ratification, negotiations were entered into with the Choctaw, Chickasaw, Cherokee, Creek and Seminole Nations which resulted in Indian Territory west of the 98th meridian being made available for the settlement of other tribes.

214   Regarding the portions of Royce Area 511 which are situated in Texas, it is urged by the defendant that the United States could not recognize title to lands which were never public lands. It is the Commission's opinion, however, that the fact that these Texas lands were never public lands would not preclude liability on the part of the United States. In the case of Lipan Apache Tribe v. United States, 180 Ct. Cl. 487, 499 (1967), involving a claim of aboriginal rather than recognized title to land in Texas, the Court of Claims held that the United States has the exclusive right to extinguish Indian title to land by its unilateral action and the fact that

Texas retained its public domain upon admission to the Union no more meant that it kept its pre-admission power over Indians than the like retention by the original States of their lands precluded the Federal Government's authority (citing Worcester v. State of Georgia, 31 U.S. (6 Pet.) 405 (1832)). Certainly, if the Federal Government may be liable for the extinguishment of an aboriginal title claim in Texas, it may be liable in a recognized title claim for its own act of purporting to grant title by treaty to Texas lands, even though it did not own the lands.

In the case of Mole Lake Band of Chippewa Indians v. United States, 134 Ct. Cl. 478, cert. denied, 352 U.S. 892 (1956), the Indians complained that the United States, when it created their reservations, granted to them areas of land including land which it had, some years before, granted to the State of Wisconsin, and that as a result of the conflicting grants the plaintiffs had been deprived of some of the land within their reservations, and of the proceeds of the timber which had been cut from these lands. The land in question had been ceded to the United States by the Chippewa Nation prior to 1850 and was public land in 1850. On September 28, 1850, Congress passed the Swamp Land Act, 9 Stat. 519. This Act provided that, in order to enable the state to construct the necessary levies and drains to reclaim the swamp lands,

> * * * the whole of those swamp and overflowed lands, made unfit thereby for cultivation, which shall remain

unsold at the passage of this act, shall be, and the same are hereby, granted to said State. (9 Stat. 519)

By the Treaty of September 30, 1854, 10 Stat. 1109, with the Chippewa Nation, the United States granted to the Chippewas certain reservations which included lands which passed to the State of Wisconsin by virtue of the Swamp Land Act. The Court found that the Indians had possession and enjoyment of the reservation lands from 1854 to the present and, therefore, had incurred no damages except for the proceeds of certain timber sales which were being held by the United States. However, in connection with the grant of lands by the United States to the Indians, the Court, at 484-485, stated as follows:

* * *

When the United States granted the reservations to the Indians in 1854, it became obligated to them to secure to them the enjoyment of the lands and of the proceeds of the lands. This was so, whether or not the United States then had good title to the lands which it purported to grant. If the title had failed and the Indians had lost the possession of the lands, the United States would have been liable to compensate them for their loss. If one with a better title had taken the timber from the lands, the United States would have had to compensate them for the timber. Whether or not the State of Wisconsin ever has owned or does now own the swamp lands in the reservations is immaterial to the question of the obligation of the United States to the Indians, under the Treaty of 1854.

* * *

The standards for determining recognized or reservation title have been set forth in numerous decisions of this Commission, the Court of Claims and the Supreme Court. In the case of Miami Tribe of Oklahoma v. United States, 146 Ct. Cl. 421, 439 (1959), the Court of Claims summarized these standards as follows:

* * *

> Where Congress has by treaty or statute conferred upon the Indians or acknowledged in the Indians the right to <u>permanently</u> occupy and use land, then the Indians have a right or title to that land which has been variously referred to in court decisions as 'treaty title', 'reservation title', 'recognized title' and 'acknowledged title.' As noted by the Commission, there exists no one particular form for such Congressional recognition or acknowledgment of a tribe's right to occupy permanently land and that right may be established in a variety of ways. <u>Tee-Hit-Ton</u> v. <u>United States</u>, 348 U.S. 272; <u>Hynes</u> v. <u>Grimes Packing Co.</u>, 337 U.S. 86; <u>Minnesota</u> v. <u>Hitchcock</u>, 185 U.S. 373.

See also <u>Minnesota Chippewa Tribe</u> v. <u>United States</u>, 161 Ct. Cl. 258, 267 (1963); <u>Sac and Fox Tribe</u> v. <u>United States</u>, 161 Ct. Cl. 189, 192-193, 315 F.2d 896, 897, <u>cert. denied</u>, 375 U.S. 921 (1963); <u>Crow Tribe of Indians</u> v. <u>United States</u>, 151 Ct. Cl. 281, 284 F.2d 361 (1960), <u>cert. denied</u>, 366 U.S. 924 (1961).

In the case of <u>Sioux Nation</u> v. <u>United States</u>, 24 Ind. Cl. Comm. 147 (1970), the Commission, at 157-159, discussed the manner of determining the interests of separate bands or tribes who had been granted recognized title to one tract of land by the same treaty. In that case, the Commission found that the most reasonable method of dividing tribal interests was by population averages near the effective date of the treaty of recognition. Alternatively, evidence as to the use of the recognized title area by the respective tribes may be weighed. See <u>Miami Tribe of Oklahoma</u> v. <u>United States</u>, <u>supra</u>, at 442.

The language in Article II of the Treaty of October 18, 1865,
supra, explicitly acknowledged in the Kiowa and Comanche Tribes and
"such other friendly tribes as have heretofore resided with said limits"
the right to "absolute and undisturbed use and occupation" of the lands
comprising Royce Areas 510 and 511. In the same Article II, the Kiowas
and Comanches agreed "to remove to and accept as their permanent home
the country embraced within said limits, whenever directed so to do by
the President of the United States, in accordance with the provisions
of this treaty ***." Interpreting the language of the treaty in the
light of the available evidence, we find such right was intended to be
permanent unless the President, acting in his discretion, chose to
alter the boundaries. We interpret the Treaty of October 18, 1865,
as recognizing title in the plaintiff tribes and "such other friendly
tribes as have heretofore resided within said limits" to Royce Areas
510 and 511. See United States v. Kickapoo Tribe of Kansas, 174 Ct.
Cl. 550, 554 (1966); compare Sac and Fox Tribe v. United States, supra.

After a careful review of the record herein and for the reasons
stated in this opinion, the Commission concludes, as a matter of law,
that the Treaty of October 18, 1865, 14 Stat. 717, was a treaty of
recognition, the effect of which was to recognize the title of the
plaintiff tribes and of other friendly tribes to Royce Areas 510 and
511. We believe that a trial of those issues raised by defendant is
unnecessary based upon our reasons set forth herein. Therefore, the
Commission will enter an appropriate order granting the motion for

summary judgment to the extent delineated in this opinion and this case will now proceed to a determination of the interests of those tribes who were granted recognized title to Royce Areas 510 and 511 by the Treaty of October 18, 1865, supra, and to a determination of all the other remaining issues bearing upon the question of defendant's liabilities herein, including the claim of the intervenors, The Wichita Tribe and Affiliated Bands and Groups of Indians.

Richard W. Yarborough, Commissioner

We Concur:

John T. Vance, Commissioner

Margaret H. Pierce, Commissioner

Brantley Blue, Commissioner

Chairman Kuykendall dissents:

My colleagues rest their decision on the fact that they find no evidence which shows that the 1867 Treaty was intended to implement the 1865 Treaty and therefore conclude that it does not do so, and on that basis find the defendant liable. They have ignored the presumption that obtains, and arrived at a conclusion which is unsupported by facts and have not considered some relevant facts which support the correct presumption.

A general statement of the rule of evidence concerning the presumption to which I refer appears in 29 Am. Jur. 2d Evidence, § 171 (1967), which says in part:

> It is presumed in the absence of evidence to the contrary not only that such public officers perform the duties of their office, but that acts within the sphere of their official duty, and purporting to be exercised in an official capacity and by public authority, were performed regularly and legally in compliance with controlling statutory provisions, and in good faith and in the exercise of sound judgment. ***

A court opinion involving a treaty between the United States and an Indian tribe and a subsequent Executive order, which made no mention of the treaty, appears in United States v. Moore, 62 F. Supp. 660, 669 (W. D. Wash. 1945) where the court held that:

> *** We must presume that President Cleveland, in promulgating the order creating the reservation, did so with an intent to carry out the provisions of the treaty.***

These principles of law are so thoroughly embedded in our legal system that there appears to be no need to labor this point. Let us now turn to some of the legislative history of the 1867 Treaty which fortifies the presumption and compels the conclusion that the 1867 cession by the plaintiffs was pursuant to the provision of the 1865 Treaty authorizing the President to set aside from time to time a portion of the tract described in said treaty for plaintiffs and other friendly tribes who had resided therein.

In 1867 what we now know as the Congressional Record was called the Congressional Globe. References to this document will be made by use of the word "Globe" followed by the page number. Such a citation refers to the Congressional Globe of the Fortieth Congress, First Session, in 1867.

On March 29, 1867, the Congress finally passed (Globe, 451, 452) and the President signed S. No. 83 which then became Chapter XIII, Laws of 1867, 15 Stat. 7. Section 6 thereof provided in part as follows:

> And all laws allowing the President, the Secretary of the Interior, or the commissioner of Indian affairs to enter into treaties with any Indian tribes are hereby repealed, and no expense shall hereafter be incurred in negotiating a treaty with any Indian tribe until an appropriation authorizing such expense shall be first made by law.

On July 8, 1867, the Senate adopted the following resolution:

> Resolved, That the Secretary of the Interior communicate to the Senate any reports made to his Department by commissioners heretofore appointed, or by superintendents or agents of Indian tribes, together with any other authentic and reliable information in his possession, touching the origin and progress of existing Indian hostilities on the frontier.
>
> He will further communicate to the Senate, as far as he can, the extent of the disaffection among the

Indian tribes; whether they are waging war as tribes
or as individuals, and if as individuals, what disposition has been or is likely to be made of the friendly
Indians formerly belonging to what are known as
hostile bands, and that he make such suggestions as
in his judgment will lead to the most speedy termina-
tion of pending hostilities and prevent Indian wars
in the future. Globe, 507.

On July 12, 1867, the Senate received a report from the Commissioner of Indian Affairs which was accompanied by a letter of transmittal from the Acting Secretary of the Department of the Interior. This letter stated that the report was in compliance with the resolution of the Senate of July 8. Globe, 623.

The following paragraphs are part of the report:

To make peace it is, in my opinion, necessary, first,
that that part of an act approved March 29, 1867, re-
pealing "all laws allowing the President, the Secretary of the Interior, or the Commissioner of Indian
Affairs to enter into treaties with any Indian tribe"
shall be repealed; otherwise there can be no binding
agreement for peace made with the hostile Indians, ***.

That the policy indicated may be of universal ap-
plication, I would respectfully recommend that a
large territory be set apart south of the southern line
of Kansas and west of Arkansas, including the present
Indian Territory and the country known as the staked
plains of Texas, and so much of New Mexico as may be
necessary, for the exclusive occupation and ultimate home
of all the Indians south of the Platte and east of
Arizona, and for the inauguration of this plan in
reference to said territory and said Indians I
respectfully ask that an appropriation be made of
$100,000.

I recommend that all necessary provisions be made
by Congress to procure at once that portion of Texas,
or so much thereof as may be necessary, lying between the western boundary of the Indian Territory
and the eastern boundary of New Mexico. Globe, 624.

The report was signed by N. G. Taylor, the then Commissioner of Indian Affairs. Globe, 624.

On July 16, 1867, Senator Henderson of Missouri who was the author of the resolution of July 8, and Chairman of the Senate Committee on Indian Affairs introduced S. No. 136, a bill to establish peace with certain hostile tribes. Globe, 655.

A constitutional problem was pointed out by Senator Harlan of Iowa. Part of what he said is as follows:

> ***I think, however, the committee have made a mistake in attempting to appoint the commissioners in the bill itself; and in connection with this suggestion I ask their attention to the provisions of the Constitution, and also to what has been the policy of the Government from the beginning. The Constitution of the United States says:
>
>> He [the President] shall have power, by and with the advice and consent of the Senate, to make treaties.
>
> I know of no instance in which Congress has attempted, through its own legislative machinery, or through the action of individuals appointed by Congress, to make a treaty, either with the Indian tribes or with foreign Powers; and I see no necessity, if it were not unconstitutional, in attempting now to depart from what has been heretofore the policy of the Government. With a view of testing the judgment of the Senate on this subject, at the proper time, if no one else shall do so, I will move to amend that section so as to authorize the President to appoint commissioners to negotiate with these Indians. Globe, 678.

Several amendments were adopted including the two shown in the following quoted portion of the debate:

Mr. Henderson. In the first section, line twelve,
after the word "discretion," the last word but one of
the line, I move to insert the words "under the direction
of the President;" so as to read:
And in their discretion, under the direction
of the President, to make and conclude with
said bands or tribes such treaty stipulations, &c.

The amendment was agreed to. Globe, 703.

The legality of Congressional appointment of treaty commissioners was discussed exhaustively. Globe, 704, 709, 710. Senator Henderson, the floor manager of the bill as well as Chairman of the Committee on Indian Affairs, expressed confidence that the amendment above quoted, adding the words "under the direction of the President" which he had proposed and which was adopted, removed the constitutional objection. Globe, 710.

The bill as amended was finally passed on July 20, 1867, Globe, 753, and was signed by the President on the same day, Globe, 755, and became Chapter XXXIII of Statutes at Large, 15 Stat. 17.

The portions of the legislative history set forth above not only lead to the inescapable conclusion that the presumption above mentioned cannot be overcome, but also leads to the inescapable conclusion that the acts of the treaty commissioners were those of the President, in whom rested the executive power to make treaties and who had the specific power to diminish the lands described in the 1865 Treaty.

The evidence also makes it clear beyond any doubt that the treaty commissioners had the 1865 Treaty in mind when they negotiated and concluded the 1867 Treaty. The Commissioner of Indian Affairs, N. G. Taylor, who was the leader of the treaty commissioners is the person who had recommended to Congress that it provide for the procurement of a large portion of

Texas for an Indian reservation. Obviously, he did so because he knew of the mistake of the 1865 treaty commissioners including a large part of Texas in the 1865 Treaty. Obviously all the 1867 treaty commissioners must have known these facts and intended that the 1867 Treaty replace the 1865 Treaty. Even if they did not know so and intend so (which would be incredible) they still must be presumed to have so known and intended, because the presumption that they did so still stands unrebutted.

The fact that the land described in the 1865 Treaty was reduced by the bilateral action of the parties in 1867 rather than by the unilateral action of the President makes no difference in the quantum of title transferred. There are, however, several obvious reasons why the latter course would have been followed, which I will point out.

The two year period between the signing of the 1865 Treaty and the signing of the 1867 Treaty, although a brief period, is included within a longer period (the tenure of President Andrew Johnson) when the animosity of Congress toward the President was the greatest this country has ever experienced. As we have seen, during the last seven months of this period the President was bereft of power to enter independently into any treaties with Indian tribes or to incur any expense in negotiating a treaty. (Act of March 29, 1867, ch. XIII,§6, 15 Stat. 7.)

During this period between the two treaties, fighting with Indians on the frontier absorbed a great amount of time, money and manpower of the nation and peace had to be made before the United States could secure an area for the Kiowas and Comanches to have for their own and the President could

225

direct them to remove thereto in accordance with Article II of the 1865 Treaty.

Small wonder that the President did not issue an Executive order reducing the area set aside for plaintiffs prior to the 1867 Treaty, and we can readily see why he would be slow to exercise any power granted to him by any prior treaty, after enactment of Chapter XIII of the Laws of 1867.

In short, neither any inaction on the part of the President nor a mere lapse of time can be deemed to have vested plaintiffs' predecessors with any greater title or rights in the property than they possessed on May 26, 1866, when the 1865 Treaty was proclaimed.

The cession by the Indians in 1867 accomplished, just as completely as could a Presidential order, the reduction in size of the area described in the 1865 Treaty. It superseded the 1865 Treaty.

The effect of the 1867 Treaty on the 1865 Treaty is the same as the effect of a subsequent statute upon a prior inconsistent statute. The prior statute is repealed by implication.

The title of the Indians to the land described in the 1865 Treaty which the defendant recognized by that treaty was the lowest order and was almost, but not quite completely defeasible. The President could, from time to time, reduce the area the Indians might occupy. They would have had no choice in the size or location of the lands upon which they could live. That is the title which was ceded by the Indians in the 1867 Treaty. It was not a marketable title.

The opinion of the majority of this Commission indicates that a result contrary to that which I have reached is required by Klamath Indians v. United States, 85 Ct. Cl. 451 (1937), aff'd. 304 U.S. 119 (1938) and they quote the following from the opinion of the Court of Claims, at 463-464:

> The defendant contends, as it did in the original case, that the Indian title to the 87,000 acres was not permanent or exclusive, merely a right to occupy the lands, and subject to termination by certain articles of the treaty of 1864. It is asserted that inasmuch as the treaty provisions set aside the delimited reservation to plaintiff Indians, they to occupy the same 'until otherwise directed by the President of the United States', the act of Congress taking the 87,000 acres was an exercise of this power.
>
> We cannot assent to the proposition. The President did not exercise any such power if he possessed it. On the contrary, Congress recognized the Indians' right to the lands and sought to pay for them. * * * (Klamath Indians v. United States, 85 Ct. Cl. 451, 463-464 (1937), aff'd. 304 U.S. 119 (1938))

In this opinion, immediately following what is quoted above, and in the same paragraph, we find this additional language:

> ***The Indians have been and now are in peaceable and undisturbed possession of the reservation, and this record discloses no single act of any character emanating from Congress or the President inimical to their ownership of the reservation.

The controlling factual differences between the two cases are plain to see. The Klamaths and other Indians had had possession of their land for 73 years and Congress had recognized their right to it. After the

227

defense of defeasible title had been asserted in the first trial of the Klamath case, (although the decision adverse to the Klamaths apparently was not based on that defense) and the Klamaths had lost that case for another reason, (namely the fact that they had previously given a release of their claim), Congress enacted another special jurisdictional Act authorizing them to sue again and eliminating the defense of prior release.

The actions of Congress determined that the Klamaths had a right of action upon which they should recover and left only the amount of recovery to be decided by the Court of Claims.

We have no such congressional action in this case. On the contrary, we have the action of Congress in ratifying the 1867 Treaty which contained the cession by plaintiffs' ancestors. The other factual differences, such as duration and character of possession, and the fact that the Klamaths never ceded their land to the United States are obvious. The Klamath case has no bearing on the instant case.

Plaintiffs have a claim pending before us for loss of their aboriginal title to an area which according to a statement of their counsel, comprises approximately one hundred million acres. They can and should prosecute this claim diligently; the same cannot be said for the instant claim.

Jerome K. Kuykendall, Chairman

BEFORE THE INDIAN CLAIMS COMMISSION

THE KIOWA, COMANCHE AND APACHE TRIBES OF INDIANS, Plaintiffs, THE WICHITA INDIAN TRIBE OF OKLAHOMA AND BANDS AND GROUPS OF INDIANS WHICH HAVE BEEN OR WHICH ARE AFFILIATED WITH THE WICHITA INDIAN TRIBE OF OKLAHOMA, INCLUDING BUT NOT LIMITED TO THE WICHITA, WACOS, KEECHIS, AND TOWACONIES, Plaintiffs and Intervenors, v. THE UNITED STATES OF AMERICA, Defendant.	Docket No. 257

ORDER GRANTING MOTION OF KIOWA, COMANCHE
AND APACHE TRIBES OF INDIANS FOR
SUMMARY JUDGMENT OF RECOGNIZED TITLE

Upon consideration of the motion of the Kiowa, Comanche and Apache Tribes, plaintiffs, for summary judgment of recognized title, filed February 13, 1970, and defendant's response thereto, and, further, upon the opinion this day entered herein, which is hereby made a part of this order, the Commission concludes as a matter of law that the Treaty of October 18, 1865, recognized the title of the plaintiff tribes and of other friendly tribes to Royce Areas 510 and 511.

IT IS THEREFORE ORDERED that the motion for summary judgment be, and the same is hereby, granted.

IT IS FURTHER ORDERED that this case proceed to a determination of the interests of those tribes who were granted recognized title to Royce Areas 510 and 511 by the Treaty of October 18, 1865, and to a determination of all the other remaining issues bearing upon the question of defendant's liabilities herein, including the claim of the intervenors, The Wichita Tribe and Affiliated Bands and Groups of Indians.

Dated at Washington, D. C., this 9th day of August, 1971.

John T. Vance, Commissioner

Richard W. Yarborough, Commissioner

Margaret H. Pierce, Commissioner

Brantley Blue, Commissioner